AF255696

DISCOVERED, NOT DESIGNED

BUILDING THINGS IN THE AGE OF COMPLEXITY

SEAN MCCLURE

To Mom and Dad

Contents

PART 3: REDEFINING KNOWLEDGE

CHAPTER 8: PROPERTIES OVER REASONS

CHAPTER 9: LIFE IS NOT A GAME

PART 4: CONSEQUENCES

CHAPTER 10: FLAWED GATEKEEPING

CHAPTER 11: VICIOUS CYCLES

Introduction

A Critical Shift

Society requires a fundamental change in mindset. One that realizes, and accepts, that the approach used to build things in today's economy is coming to an end. This approach, regardless of any derivative name it might go by, is *design*. Humans have designed their creations since the beginning of our history. To design is to choose the pieces and interactions that produce the outputs needed to solve problems. These choices can be placed into plans or drawings, instructing others how to make things.

The stone axe came to be thanks to the human ability to mix our physical intuitions about the world with distinct discoveries related to carving wood, shaping stone and binding plant fibers. For almost all human history, discovery alone was never enough to produce useful things. Only by harnessing our discoveries through design were we able to piece together our epiphanies into causal chains of functionality.

Design does wonders when the things we build are deterministic. Something is deterministic when the same inputs always give the same outputs. The input to the stone axe is the force of our hand, which is then transferred to the wooden handle, through its length, into the fibrous binding and finally to the sharp edge where the output is delivered. If you wield an axe, you cut the material. Of course, countless errors could creep into this activity. You might lose your grip, or a gust of wind could veer your blade away from the target. But the object itself is fully deterministic because it consists of an exact causal chain of actions, transferred from one piece to the next, until the output is produced. This is no different from the office building, the bridge, the internal combustion engine or the rocket. Problems solved, thanks largely to design.

But design actively interferes with the process of creating things that are complex. Complex things are nothing like the stone axe, the office building, the bridge, the internal combustion engine or the rocket. Complex things are the stuff of nature. Where the engine has cogs and pistons, nature's solutions are wet, smooth and organic. Nature does not push pieces into pieces to produce her outputs. Nature does not craft machines of causality. Nature's solutions are adaptive, resilient and above all emergent.

Complex things have nondeterministic aspects to them, which means the same inputs do not always give the same outputs. This lack of exactness is the essence of complexity. But as we will see, it is not one of increased difficulty relative to things not complex, it is a different beast altogether. Complex things do not produce their outputs from deterministic steps, rather they materialize what is needed in some other fashion. This *other fashion* is a major topic of this book. Nature's approach to creation cannot be explained by reductionist science. Emergence flies in the face of how today's scientists and engineers put forward most of their explanations and build their systems.

Critically, emergence cannot be reverse engineered and placed into a plan. Nondeterministic objects lack the precision and control that has been the mainstay of traditional engineering since humans began building. This has made complexity-avoidance a core part of how humans now build things at scale. By avoiding complexity, we look to prevent errors from creeping in and destroying the reliability of our systems. If the stone axe cannot be gripped properly, or gets pushed too easily by the wind, it is useless at best, risky at worst.

Without this control over outputs the premise of design flies out the window. The choice of pieces and their connections, and any plan those might be placed into, no longer speak to how a thing works. A design is only worth what it can control. Design demands strict determinism in the things it envisions. One must be able to see how pieces interact with other pieces for a design to be made; to reason about how a chain of events leads to something definite.

But emergence cannot be designed because emergence is not about inner causality. Emergence, while still about producing outputs that solve problems, does not align to the simplistic notion of things-bumping-into-things. The underlying mechanisms of emergence do not appear as mechanisms at all, not in the traditional sense. While emergence manifests itself through the collective action of pieces, it looks nothing like those pieces. Design is the very antithesis of everything emergence stands for.

Complex things are what we now must create to solve today's challenges. We are entering a stage in human history where the things we build are becoming *necessarily* complex. The necessity of complexity comes from the fact that only complex things solve truly hard problems. Hard problems do not mean difficult; such notions are a byproduct of looking at complexity through the incorrect lens of simple systems; a misunderstanding of the difference between simple and complex. Complexity is not an extension of simple systems; it is altogether different. A hard problem is only more challenging if one erroneously attempts to solve it using the approaches for simple problems. Hard problems are categorically different from the kind solved by the stone axe, the office building, the bridge, the internal combustion engine or the rocket. Hard problems demand a completely different kind of solution.

To build in this coming *age of complexity* we will need to engineer emergence into the systems we build. Engineering emergence sounds oxymoronic to the traditional engineer. For what would it mean to craft something whose internals cannot be reasoned about? How would one envision the look and feel of something that manifests on its own? How can one make sense of a system whose outputs look nothing like the pieces from which it is composed? And yet, this is precisely what must be accomplished.

This changes almost everything. Beyond just a new paradigm of science and engineering, the need to engineer emergence forces us to redefine meritocracy and the preceding definition of skill such notions of excellency depend on. The implications are extensive. Everything comes down to building things. We build not just technologies, but also institutions, cultural norms and values, social networks, knowledge and education systems, economic systems, political structures, social support systems and ethical and legal frameworks. The need to engineer emergence precludes the foundation that undergirds almost all narratives in science, engineering and our economy.

Ultimately, the age of complexity will bring us full circle, by forcing humans to embrace the natural skills we evolved for; those that have been denigrated by the so-called Enlightenment and the needs of the Industrial Revolution. The world has pathologized the messiness of human bias and our reliance on heuristics. This disparaging perspective is a byproduct of the simple systems we built throughout history, where low-dimensional thinking proved to be an excellent ally. But such simplistic framing betrays what works under complexity. Our soft biases and messy heuristics evolved because they are how truly hard problems are solved.

Humans evolved as they have because knowledge of details does not map to producing outputs that solve hard problems. Society has been told to downplay human emotion as some weaker form of reasoning, when in fact the best reason emerges from an intense desire to follow one's evolutionary emotional cues. This is not some appeal to the softer side of humanity, or some grudge against rationality; quite the opposite. It is a definite stand against the hubris, and intellectual dishonesty, of telling nature she got it wrong.

The current scientific and engineering paradigm is rooted in the notion of design; the idea that we can reverse engineer nature, look upon its parts, explain how things work and use those explanations to create a plan. We use designs to orient the efforts of millions of people by division of labor. Designs are what today's notions of knowledge and skill rest on. Without designs we would not know what to work on, how to fix things, or how to think of systems as reliable. To know something, we are told, is to know the *inner workings* of the phenomena that inspire us, and anything we build hence from.

Almost every technological thing humans have built has been mechanistic and deterministic. This is because the mechanical and electronic things we have created have all been, by definition, simple. Simple here does not mean easy to find, it means that the physical solution created to solve the challenge produces its outputs in a deterministic fashion. Simple objects use a basic set of causally connected steps to produce their outputs. Such constructs cannot solve categorically hard problems. Simple things solve simple problems. Complex things solve hard problems.

Nature's solutions solve the hardest problems of all. These *naturally hard problems* are presented within natural environments, and resolved, not by converting inputs into outputs using a simplistic blend of parts, but by the realization of emergent structures. Naturally hard problems do not fit neatly into the "complexity classes" of computer science, or any other classifications used to denote a problem's degree of difficulty. Naturally hard problems cannot be solved by breaking it into pieces and solving parts in isolation. Nature is not subject to the contrived, low-dimensional approaches of human engineering. Only the existence of a truly complex object can bring about a solution to a naturally hard problem.

Solutions that solve naturally hard problems have a physical makeup that is fundamentally different from what humans have traditionally built. The number of pieces and interactions inside complex solutions number well beyond the machines of human creation. But therein lies a commonality between human engineering and nature. Increasing the number of pieces to solve greater challenges has been part of human technological progress since our beginning.

Let us start our journey there, with humanity's continual stringing-together of pieces, in its quest to reach higher, farther and faster.

PART 1
SOLVING BY BUILDING

Chapter 1

Progress by Abstraction

More and More Pieces

As we reach higher, farther and faster with our technologies we attempt to solve more difficult challenges. Concomitant with this increased difficulty is the addition of more pieces to what we build. More pieces are required because that is how we account for the additional factors present inside challenging situations. Imagine a bridge that spans a small river. Such an object requires a few core parts to ensure its integrity. But start building bridges that span wide rivers and the game changes. Now we need more foundations, columns and beams to support and distribute the load correctly. More segments, sections and decking materials ensure numerous vehicles and pedestrians traverse safely. Additional joints and bearings account for thermal expansion, wind-induced movements and seismic activity.

This is the nature of difficult problems. They have more factors that must be attended to using additional pieces. We can see problem difficulty reflected in the solutions we have created throughout history. The things we build today have far more pieces than anything created in the past. A single modern passenger jet has over a million parts. Our electrical grids contain millions of points of connection. Our satellites are composed of an intricate array of antennas, solar panels and propulsion mechanisms. Automobiles are now loaded with advanced technologies and components designed to enhance performance, safety and convenience. There are billions of transistors on a single microchip. Harder problems demand more pieces.

One would assume that more details inside the things we build commands more requisite knowledge of how they work. It seems like anyone building something today would need to know much more than those who came before. Whatever knowledge a bridge builder from 200 years ago required, just imagine how much one needs today.

But this poses a question. How are humans creating such increasing sophistication in mere generations? How can all the pieces be held within a single mind? Are people just getting smarter? Are we working harder? We know this is not the case. The human brain has not changed in 50,000 years, and modern man most definitely does not work harder. How are we making such astounding progress without more intelligence or effort?

The fact is, technological progress would never happen if it required human knowledge to keep pace with the increasing levels of intricacy in our inventions. The reason humans can advance technologically is because each generation begins with a more advanced starting point. Today's generation only needs to understand how to operate at the current level of progress. Human ingenuity is bootstrapped. We continuously improve and refine our inventions by using the outputs from the last generation as the inputs to the next generation. Progress is not about smarter people or better ideas; it is about automatic and inevitable advancement achieved by folding preceding work into new beginnings. Only by packaging the details of today's solutions into easier to use tools does humanity move forward. Human progress is thus a story about abstraction.

Higher and Higher

Consider the vast improvements in software that have occurred over the last 50 years. This is a story of making it easier to do the same thing with less code. It all began with the most exhausting way to do this; machine code. Machine code consists of binary instructions processed directly by computer hardware. Imagine trying to instruct a robot to navigate a maze. We cannot use words like "walk" or "turn left" since this is not information a robot can use. Only strings of zeros and ones will do.

Machine code represents the instructions that sit closest to the microchip, and is thus the lowest level of abstraction. Operating at the lowest level of abstraction takes the most time for a given task, since each instruction performs a very basic operation. It is like trying to build a house from raw materials instead of using prefabricated pieces.

One step higher in abstraction is assembly language, which can be thought of as a human-readable version of machine code. Assembly language uses symbols more familiar to humans, which eases reading and speeds up the task of instructing a machine. We can think of assembly language as an interface that sits on top of machine code. This interface allows programmers to more rapidly achieve what took the previous generation much longer. This is because for every one "lever" you pull in assembly language multiple levers get pulled in machine code.

Continuing up the ladder of abstraction we have procedural programming. Such languages enable programmers to instruct the machine using named procedures and functions. These are akin to chunks of prepackaged assembly language, bringing forth a yet-higher level of abstraction. By packaging up assembly language into chunks, programmers could now think of computer functionality in terms of reusable modules. Now our house-building materials come partially assembled, making it easier to put together our home.

When it comes to building software, more difficult challenges require bigger teams and better communication. Different requirements must be managed and folded into the development process. Teams must explore more possibilities and iterate more prototypes to achieve what is needed. This makes procedural programming too cumbersome for many modern applications. Enter the next generation, which rises above procedural languages with object-oriented programming (OOP). This innovation abstracts away the low-level details that were present in procedural programming, introducing concepts like objects, which encapsulate data and behavior into even higher-level reusable components.

With OOP our house-building pieces are even more prebuilt. OOP brings computing constructs that are more aligned to how humans think about the world. Concepts like inheritance, polymorphism and encapsulation make creating software a higher-level concern. Consider how prefabricated building supplies makes home-building a more strategic and creative act, as one is no longer mired in the weeds of extreme details. At the industrial scale, it means more focus on optimizing efficiency, quality control, scalability and sustainability. With OOP, the "chunking" of functionality that began with assembly language was now reaching a level of modularity and extensibility that made computer programming faster, and far more accessible to people interested in computing.

But why stop there? People want dynamic web applications like online shopping sites, social media platforms, online banking services, learning and collaboration tools, travel and booking websites, gaming systems, healthcare and job portals, and various online marketplaces. Scripting languages became crucial here, making it possible to develop interactive and dynamic user interfaces. Challenges like asynchronous operations, event handling and browser compatibility compelled the arrival of languages even more abstract. By bringing more simplicity and readability to how humans instruct machines, things like memory management and pointer arithmetic were abstracted away, replaced with dynamic typing, extensive libraries and a large community and ecosystem to support rapid development. With scripting, the gap between ideation and working software continued to close.

At the highest level of abstraction are visual and audio interfaces. The Graphical User Interface (GUI) abstracts away the inner details of machine interaction by providing visual representations of the underlying data and functionality. There are now drag-and-drop tools for putting together software, and with the incorporation of artificial intelligence (AI) into building tools, completely codeless development is becoming a reality. Even those with disabilities can now write code using voice commands.

Today, entire applications can be prototyped in weeks. The organization of labor that makes this possible looks much different than it did 50 years ago. Many non-technical individuals now play vital roles in making today's software products a reality. The demarcation between technical and nontechnical professionals is breaking down, blended by the high levels of abstraction achieved in today's software development tools.

This means the kind of challenges that can now be resolved with software far surpass anything previous generations could have tackled. We can now analyze massive amounts of data like never before. We can build machines that show some form of intelligence, performing tasks like speech recognition, image classification and natural language processing. We now create advanced climate models, analyze and correlate patient records, explore distant planets, study cosmic phenomena and connect people globally through video conferencing.

What started as a niche experiment has become arguably the biggest player in our economy. Software brings forth collaboration and human connectivity on an unprecedented scale. And this was, and is, possible thanks to the power of increasing levels of abstraction. Each generation has been presented with the means to piece together software more easily than the generation before, and that means solving harder problems than the previous generation. It means being able to manage and control the increasing number of pieces that must be brought to bear on harder problems.

Abstraction does not remove details, rather it subsumes them into higher-level constructs that allow many pieces to be operated using fewer levers. Abstraction makes progress inevitable, because it pushes human ingenuity forward by packaging details and creating interfaces; interfaces that are the starting points for the next generation.

When we look around and see skyscrapers, satellites, supercomputers, high-speed trains, nuclear power plants, smartphones, computers and biomedical implants, it is hard to imagine humans could create such apparent sophistication. The inner workings of the objects humans have created are highly detailed, require intricate coordination and timing, and all things considered, are quite reliable. But when we realize that each generation needs only to use the previous generation as its starting point, the way progress occurs becomes clear. Builders within a generation do not require knowledge of how everything works, they must only comprehend their current level of abstraction.

This means the overwhelming amount of knowledge regarding the inner workings of things is not held by anyone alive today. Such knowledge has been obfuscated by the ongoing levels of increasing abstraction each generation adds to their creations. This is true for all areas of human innovation. Today's humans are not smarter than our ancestors. We do not work harder. We do not even know that much more. Human advancement is best understood as an ongoing story of increased abstraction and bootstrapped progress.

Physical Abstraction

Abstraction is usually thought about in the context of cognition. Humans create high-level concepts that are derived from the usage and classification of specific examples. By choosing to combine specifics into a single category we are implementing abstraction. To say that all dog breeds fit into the category "dog" is to create the abstraction *dog*. To make an abstract painting is to envision only the necessary, undetailed parts needed to produce an impression. Abstraction in the mind is how humans comprehend and navigate their complex environments, by lowering the cognitive load necessary to maneuver through the details of life.

One might assume that abstraction is a purely informational phenomenon. After all, the higher-level constructs brought about by each generation of computer programmers are chunks of information, interacted with on an informational level. To create a module in programming is akin to creating the category "dog" in human language. It is an activity that lowers the cognitive load necessary to wield the immense number of details inside software.

But abstraction can also be physical. The house-building analogy was not just an analogy. If one uses larger prebuilt pieces as their starting points they are operating with abstractions. Just as the mind can combine specifics into a single category, so too can physical details be combined to serve a singular function at a higher level.

We can understand physical abstraction by looking at how humans make things usable. Nobody would have used the stone axe if they had to hold the blade against the handle while swinging it. The binding used combines the blade and handle into a single object, alleviating any need on the user's part to consider their attachment. Things are only usable if the effort required to operate them is lower than what would be required if each piece had to be coordinated manually.

Consider the automobile. If drivers were required to manually coordinate all the inner workings of the internal combustion engine, the chassis and the transmission, nobody could drive a car. The interfaces that are provided to a driver have far less details than the inner workings of the machine. Even the stick shift in a manual transmission is a physical abstraction. It achieves what all abstractions do; provides an interface that decreases the number of levers one must pull to accomplish a task. With a stick shift a driver can select the desired gear by moving only a lever and clutch, eliminating the need to physically engage each gear within the gearbox. The clearly marked gear positions are an interface, one that enables the driver to make a selection without having to navigate through a series of internal details. Of course, automatic transmission takes physical abstraction to the next level, allowing us to operate gears with little consideration for how they work internally.

Just as we mentally combine disparate things into single categories, the stick shift represents a single physical construct that encompasses a set of inner physical details, while the automatic transmission takes this even higher (thanks to a subsequent generation). The physical version of abstraction that accompanies human ingenuity is a critical part of human progress.

The set of best practices that are implemented within a given industry or profession are structured around the physical abstractions we create. The MRI technician is not coordinating the magnetization, RF pulse excitation, signal detection, data acquisition and image reconstruction. The barista is not manually heating water, building pressure, grinding beans, extracting flavors or producing steam. The asphalt paver is not sourcing stone, gravel and sand, nor experimenting with binders. Professionals in any field are operating above the level of previously worked-out details via physical abstraction. This means our notions of knowledge and skill are fully aligned to physical abstractions, as they are the starting points people use to operate the systems in their field.

All of human progress is a story of moving humanity forward without requiring more knowledge or effort than the previous generation. But as automatic and inevitable as such progress is, creating interfaces requires deliberate thinking. Making physical abstractions is an intentional act that calls upon long and careful consideration. The physical abstractions created by humans have historically been made possible by design.

Abstraction by Design

The most obvious way to create physical abstractions is through design. We can make conscious decisions regarding what pieces to include, how to connect them and how to expose their underlying functionality through an interface. In the computing example, procedural programming came about by making deliberate decisions regarding how to bundle pieces of machine code into higher level syntax and semantics. This requires calculated reasoning. One must reach into the guts of their current abstraction level and decide how to connect and expose those pieces into a higher level. Design creates physical abstractions by way of packaging the inner workings of an object. This groups disparate functionalities into single constructs at a higher level. It is this bundling that allows the disparate functionalities inside a system to be coordinated more easily from the outside.

This shows us that the informational and physical versions of abstraction are deeply connected. The deliberate reasoning used in design has us noticing the shared characteristics of some group of disparate things. The stick shift works because it connects to a set of lower-level, internal pieces that share a common purpose. Such a physical construct has been achieved by using our mental capacity to notice patterns, and group those patterns into higher-level form. Physical abstraction is a reflection of the conscious abstractions we make with our minds.

We can see that humans achieve their technological progress via abstraction, and that abstraction can be realized by design. This has made design a core part of our historical progress. But design comes with a cost, for one cannot design without witnessing *how* the internal pieces of a system bump into each other.

Design Depends on Determinism

To design is to reason about explicit connections made between lower and higher levels of abstraction. This is why design depends on determinism. Design only works when we can assess how the outputs of a system are produced, in the deterministic sense. We cannot bundle the inner workings of a transmission into a higher-level stick shift unless we can see how different gears affect each other. We cannot bundle the C language into C++ modules unless we can see how the C language works explicitly. This underlies the entire justification for design. If we could not reason about how each internal piece interacts to produce outputs, our designs would be little more than guesswork and supposition.

One might be tempted to suggest that design could in fact be high level itself. Could not design be a general set of guidelines that help coax efforts in a positive direction? Would this not make design disconnected from a strict sense of determinism? But that is not design, that is a methodology or framework. Frameworks are overarching principles that help keep people on track to achieve certain goals. Such things do not reach into the system and reason about its internals. To design is to make intentional choices about how different elements interact and relate to each other. Design depends fully on the premise of deterministic knowledge.

Determinism relates to systems or processes whose behavior is entirely predictable based on its inputs and the rules governing its operation. If you give the same initial inputs to a deterministic system again and again, it will always produce the same outputs. This notion of repeatability, predictability and absence of randomness is baked into the notion of design. Design operates under the assumption that there are a set of explicit steps that flow from input to output.

If this were not the case, then choosing specific pieces and connections would be futile.

It is important to distinguish, again, between deterministic and nondeterministic systems/processes. A nondeterministic system is one whose behavior is not entirely predictable. Unlike deterministic systems, which produce the same output for a given set of inputs every time, nondeterministic systems can be expected to produce different behaviors or outcomes, even when provided with the same inputs and initial conditions. The same set of cars and drivers, driving at the same speeds, arriving at an intersection with no stop signs or traffic lights, will not produce purely predictable traffic flow. There will be a great deal of variation in the sequence of movements and flow of vehicles. A system that produces different outcomes, despite being provided the same inputs, cannot be designed.

Some readers might pause here, proclaiming that the previous example must be wrong. For we know that traffic systems can indeed be designed, and they obviously add predictable behavior to the flow of traffic. But this is not designing the traffic itself, this is designing an outer framework that governs a nondeterministic system (traffic). Current traffic systems do not attempt to control the specific interactions between vehicles, they merely place external limitations that apply to all vehicles. This is akin to a government creating frameworks that regulate free markets. Any attempt to design the system itself, such as dictating the specific interactions between cars or between customers and sellers, can be expected to interfere with the functioning of a nondeterministic system.

Determinism Cannot Solve Hard Problems

Nondeterminism is directly related to how difficult a problem is. Just as one cannot design (internally) a nondeterministic system, hard problems cannot be solved by determinism. Hard problems, as we will see in chapter 4, are problems that require trial-and-error and heuristics to solve. As stated in the introduction, a hard problem is not something that is more challenging relative to simple problems, rather it is a categorically distinct situation that demands a very different kind of solution.

We can understand just how different a solution must be when it comes to solving hard problems by looking at nature. As already stated, nature's solutions solve the hardest problems of all. These *naturally hard problems* are presented by natural environments, and are resolved by objects that do not convert inputs into outputs using a simplistic blend of deterministically-connected pieces. Nature solves its challenges via the realization of emergent structures. This means nature does not create solutions that have well-defined steps between inputs and outputs. Such a construct could not resolve naturally hard problems because nature's situations are made of countless factors and interactions that define them. It is not a matter of collecting enough rules to account for nature's intricacy; in fact, it is not a game of rules at all. Even if we could fashion an object with a rule for every possible contingency it would fail to solve a hard problem.

Thinking of hard problems as if they are more difficult versions of rules-based systems is akin to trying to describe quantum mechanics using classical mechanics. A classical description is not remotely close to what is happening, because the quantum realm is fundamentally not classical. It is not a matter of degree or approximation, it is a matter of being an entirely different thing altogether.

Nature's solutions harbor true complexity, which means its outputs are not a product of summed interactions or a path of sequential procedures. Nature creates configurations of matter that produce the outputs needed in an entirely different fashion than rules-based processing. We will look into this different mechanism later, but for now, it is critical to appreciate that nature's solutions are fundamentally different from the simple systems produced by humans. Not only do nature's solutions have a great deal of nondeterminism to them, but they also *require* that nondeterminism to function as they do.

Consider facial recognition; a feat performed naturally by humans and advanced AI systems. What makes facial recognition a hard problem is not just the sheer number of factors related to the phenomenon, but that the very word "solve" means something different than our usual deterministic framing. Under determinism, *solve* means what it does in mathematics, which is to find a specific, definitive answer or set of answers. But nondeterministic systems are more akin to the notion of probabilistic answers, with some degree of correctness; a softer version of what we see in determinism.

But while this softness analogy is closer to the spirit of nondeterminism, it still frames nondeterminism as an approximate version of what we see in deterministic systems. For example, most computational approaches that seek a solution to computationally hard problems use techniques like optimization to find a satisfactory or acceptable outcome that meets certain criteria or objectives. But, as I will argue later, the idea that nondeterminism is a second-rate or approximate version of determinism is incorrect.

The solving that happens under complexity is not a weaker or more approximate solution, but rather a completely different type of solution altogether. Moreover, the type of solution found under complexity is far more powerful and realistic than anything that a precise and deterministic solution could be. The very notion of approximation is just another byproduct of thinking about complex things incorrectly, through the lens of simplicity. Genuine solutions to hard problems do not approximate, they compute directly the answer needed by using a fundamentally different notion of computing. The severe distinction between running a mathematical calculation and solving a real-world problem will be expounded on later.

The lack of causal mechanisms at the heart of complexity precludes any chance of design being able to produce the kind of solutions that make complexity tractable. There are no bundles that can be created to expose deterministically connected interfaces to users. Design's dependence on determinism means design can only find solutions to categorically simple problems.

This brings us to a critical crossroads posed by our historical approach to solving problems by building things: 1) We need to create physical abstractions to make progress, 2) the creation of physical abstractions has always been done by design, 3) design cannot solve hard problems, and 4) hard problems are what we now must solve with the things we build.

The current way we create physical abstractions will soon come to an end. Design cannot create the things we need to build solutions. The inherent complexity in the situations we now face demand something that design cannot deliver. We cannot reason about the pieces and the connections, because the mechanism by which nature's solutions solve problems is inherently different.

It has always been a kind of misplaced concreteness to talk of nature as though she is some deterministic machine. Sometimes it is merely a naive way to look at the world, other times this transgression plays out dangerously in society and politics. But now, the notion that nature is akin to rules-based machinery directly hinders progress. Only by dramatically reframing what it means to build things will the future remain tractable.

The fundamental change in problem class, and the solutions needed to resolve them, undergirds the philosophical shift required to operate effectively in the age of complexity. The challenge is not one of merely accepting the degradation of causal understanding, it is redefining our concepts of knowledge, skill, and our approach to human innovation. We have to build differently.

Abstraction is Required for Progress

Not being able to continue progress via design does not negate the fact that abstraction is required for progress. A more difficult problem cannot be solved by merely connecting more pieces together into a different object. Pieces must be bundled into higher-level constructs for the next generation to use. This is how a large number of pieces get placed into more intricate objects correctly. It is too computationally demanding to arrange thousands or millions of pieces individually, deliberately and with the correct coordination. Lower-level pieces must find the informational cohesion necessary to solve the problem one level higher, and abstraction is how this cohesion is achieved.

This is true for any notion of progress. Consider how the human mind creates abstractions to understand our world. We cannot navigate through life without placing what we see and hear into higher-level entities. If we could not categorize things as threats versus opportunities, friends versus foes, food, danger, shelter, etc. then we could not survive. By creating mental abstractions in the mind, that subsume superficially different things into single categories, we dramatically lower the cognitive load necessary to maneuver through life.

This ability to spot connections between different things extends into all our innovations. Everything from new philosophies to new technologies come about because we can bind both information and physical things into new entities. It is abstraction that makes difficult challenges computationally feasible, because abstraction is what produces new informational and physical structures that compute, without needing a one-to-one matching between a problem's detail and a solution's procedure. It is abstraction that arranges things such that the necessary internal coordination of pieces can attend to the multitude of factors inside harder challenges. In short, there is no progress without abstraction.

This is as true for nature as it is for humans. Nature progresses via its process of change and development over time. Nature's solutions continually solve problems against shifting environmental stressors. If we step back and look at human innovation overall, this is a problem being solved by nature, since humans are organisms that interact en-masse to solve problems. But when it comes to our specific inventions, humans create their new abstractions by design, as already discussed. The pieces that are placed together are done so deliberately, using causal information about how those pieces interact. This cannot be how nature creates her abstractions. Nature is not using conscious reasoning to bind pieces into higher-level constructs. And yet nature solves problems that are far more difficult than anything man tackles with his bridges and rocket engines.

This poses a critical question. If progress by abstraction is a universal property, harbored by any system that evolves to solve harder problems, how is nature creating her abstractions?

Physical abstraction, in both cases, is still the bundling together of functionality into higher-level groups and exposing an interface, but the bundle in nature is not some deterministically designed aggregation, it is a statistically automatic manifestation of matter. If this all sounds too hand-wavy, rest assured the remainder of this book will describe what I mean. But what matters at this juncture is the admission that nature's physical abstractions, while critical for progress, are not designed. There is no conscious effort by nature to choose which pieces and interactions constitute a bundle, and so abstraction in nature must have a fundamentally different mechanism.

This raises the question: how does nature "know" what pieces to combine into higher-level constructs if it cannot reason about which pieces to include, and how to connect them? How does nature create its bundles? How can the mindless process of natural selection spot the similarities that connect one level of matter in service to the next?

Chapter 2

Hitting the Wall

Progress Absent Design

At this point we have seen how humans make progress. Not by getting smarter, working harder or thanks to so-called geniuses. It is through the progressive act of designing higher and higher levels of abstraction. A given generation can solve the same problems as the previous ones, but faster, since their starting points have been advanced forward. But design depends on determinism, and determinism cannot solve truly hard problems; the kind of problems we now want/need to build solutions for. The number of factors and interactions that must be attended to by our creations are far greater than anything a rules-based paradigm can address.

We are left with a serious question. How can humanity continue to make technological progress if we can no longer design our solutions? How can we reason about the things we must build if there is no causality to uncover, no detailed set of steps to implement, and no notion of inner knowledge of the systems we create? How can the next generation be given new starting points if we cannot deliberately fashion interfaces to wield an increasing number of details?

We have hit a wall in terms of progress by abstraction. As argued in the previous chapter, progress by abstraction is a universal truth. All systems require them to make any notion of progress. The only way to continue pushing the boundaries of abstraction is to find a new way to do so; a way that does not rely on design. Such an alternative mode of construction must exist inside natural systems, since nature could not progress without doing so.

Nature is defined, above all, by its complexity, which tells us that complexity is necessary going forward. More to the point, complexity is what we must build. We cannot make progress by merely increasing complication. It is not a matter of just adding more pieces, it is about achieving genuine complexity.

Hitting the wall on design means landing on our creative limit under the current paradigm. There is no moving forward with simple machines crafted through simplistic reasoning. As counterintuitive as it will seem to many, the newness we require is the oldest process around. It is the mindless process used by nature that holds the key to the complex realm. But the cost of embracing this approach is unfathomable to many. Giving up on the supposed enlightened thinking of our reductionist past seems like the only way forward. Yet it is nature's thoughtless and unreasoned mechanisms that bind disparate parts into common functionality; the abstractions that compute answers to hard problems. This is what we must learn to build.

But this natural way of building cannot be some random effort to mash things together haphazardly, hoping for the best. Our efforts must work within the feasibility of problem solving, and the space of possibilities that harbors a problem's solution. The conundrum posed by the necessity of complexity seems to run directly against how humans use their minds to solve problems.

But not everything humans have built conforms to the reductionist and deterministic framing. Humans have brought about things whose outputs are produced not solely by their intended designs. There are things like societies, markets and certain technologies that work thanks to something not deliberately placed there by design. This means humans have the capacity to create things as nature, providing hints as to how we might continue progress by abstraction, absent design.

Hints at Building Complexity

Humans have made a few things that compare to nature in sophistication. Of course, the word "made" must be taken with a grain of salt. We are not talking about systems that have been designed, rather systems that have become what they are unintentionally. Objects that were not so much engineered as they were arrived at, using something beyond what was originally set in place. These objects verge on true complexity, not only because they have many pieces and interactions, but because many of their critical outputs are produced by mechanisms we never created.

The closest we have come to creating true complexity, what we see in nature, are things like cities, financial systems, electrical grids, the internet and artificial intelligence systems. What makes these objects enter the realm of true complexity is that their outputs are not solely produced by deliberate engineering. These objects all show the early signs of what we call emergence, meaning the appearance of structures and behaviors that do not exist in the pieces from which they are made.

Consider electrical grids, which show voltage fluctuations, power oscillations and frequency deviations that were not engineered into the system. These behaviors are not gremlins in the machine, or byproducts of intricacy whose complexity must be tolerated. Electrical grids work thanks largely to their emergent properties. A grid's stability is possible because of its self-organizing nature. Electrical grids have demonstrated built-in resilience to equipment failures, natural disasters, and cyber-attacks, by dynamically adapting to disruptions and rerouting power flows. Networks can naturally isolate affected areas and restore functionality through redundant systems. While the creation of multiple redundant pathways for power transmission is indeed a deliberate effort, the self-healing and natural isolation of affected areas arise from the *interaction* of these engineered components, not from explicit human control.

Cities do not exist solely through planning and deliberate decision making. Any large city owes its form and function to self-organizing behavior. Consider where businesses locate themselves based on countless possible variables, such as changes in accessibility, customer demographics and dynamic competition. The formation of a commercial district can arise in highly unpredictable fashion. Street patterns and building densities emerge from the cumulative effects of geographical constraints mixed with individual decisions, rather than central planning alone. Cities are hubs of economic activity, where goods, services, labor, and real estate operate interdependently, producing the structures and behaviors that give cities their look and feel. As citizens interact organically, we see pockets of community cohesion, and public transportation systems born out of unplanned traffic patterns and unforeseen mobility demands.

Our financial systems are a result of the mixing between entities, instruments and market participants. The collective actions of investors, traders and institutions bring about market prices, trading volumes and volatility that are largely unforeseen. Patterns of supply and demand, investor sentiment and information dissemination all mix and match to produce this thing we call a market. The determination of prices is not so determined after all, rather they arise from the aggregation of diverse opinions, beliefs and trading strategies. The ever-evolving regulatory frameworks emerge from the blending of needs and priorities, bringing built-in stability and integrity to the system. Our financial systems can (usually) withstand shocks, disruptions and stresses; a resilience that was never engineered into the system.

The internet brings about the formation of opinions and collective decision-making, thanks to the electronic aggregation and dissemination of diverse opinions, beliefs and knowledge. As a decentralized network of interconnected devices, the internet showcases the telltale signs of complexity such as network scalability, resilience and adaptability. Online communities and social networks emerge spontaneously, as users engage in discussions, collaborations, and collective actions. The democratization of content creation and distribution has led to the emergence of viral content, memes, trends and even cultural movements.

Of course, such emergent behavior can also work against us. Electrical grids can take a minor voltage fluctuation or frequency deviation and turn it into a cascading blackout. There are bubbles, crashes and feedback amplifications that can destabilize markets. This is the cost of complexity. What makes complex things work can also produce outputs unfavorable to our refined use cases. The point is, these behaviors were not deliberately engineered into the system, and none of these systems would work the way they do without their emergent properties.

Arguably the most complex thing humans have created are our current AI systems, or more specifically the models that drive them. These are based on machine learning techniques, specifically deep learning. Deep learning converts raw data into intelligent outputs like natural language conversation and facial recognition. But how this conversion takes place is not known, at least not in the usual manner scientists and engineers explain things. No researcher or engineer understands how the inputs given to AI systems are converted into the outputs that make its version of intelligence possible. This is because AI is not programmed the way traditional software is. While the scaffolding of AI systems is indeed rules-based, the inner details that bring about intelligent outputs are much more akin to how electrical grids, cities and financial markets produce their most important outputs.

To understand how deep learning works, we first must redefine what we mean by "how things work." The *how* in our explanation cannot be a deterministic set of steps that show information being transformed in a specific fashion. Instead, engineers can only program the outer scaffolding that puts in place a process that eventually converges to what is needed.

The most straightforward, albeit loose, analogy to describing what AI is doing rests on the notion of fitting a line to data. This is a common approach in science used to find something deeper than the data alone. When we fit a line to data, we are attempting to find a general trend that might give us some predictive ability regarding the system of interest. Say we are plotting temperature against ice cream sales. Plotting those values and searching for a trend would likely produce a line showing that higher temperatures correspond to more ice cream sales.

With this line in hand, we are now in possession of something that can presumably predict ice cream sales. We can look at the temperature tomorrow and read off the amount of ice cream we are likely to sell at that temperature. In fact, we don't need the plot at all. Since we fitted a line to data, and a line can be depicted as a mathematical expression, we have a *function*. A function is something that maps inputs to outputs, allowing us to produce a value from a given input. In our ice cream example, we can plug in the temperature on a given day and out pops a value for the amount of ice cream we can expect to sell.

This notion of fitting a line to data to arrive at a function cannot be too unlike what our mind is doing when it learns about the world. Of course, the mind is not using simplistic lines through some low-dimensional plot of values, but the high-level concept is the same. We encounter our world via our senses, which is akin to collecting data. These data are the raw inputs we use to fashion mental models about how things work and what they mean. When children first learn to speak, they are developing internal latent models related to grammar, vocabulary and sentence structure. The "function" they learn converts inputs (the sounds we hear) into outputs (the meaning of the words).

All of life is akin to learning functions, even if those functions are purely in the abstract sense. When we interact with others we pick up on social dynamics, and use our expectations of behavior, norms and social cues to navigate through complex situations. It is our mental models of these situations that enable us to predict others' reactions to what we say and do. When we drive a car, we are implementing our models of the road layout, traffic patterns and the behavior of other drivers. We anticipate potential hazards and make decisions about speed, direction and timing. None of this would be possible without a set of internal functions that map inputs to outputs. To learn anything is to "fit lines" to sensory data to create models of the world around us.

Building a model, like a line, requires finding parameters, since it is parameters that give models their form. Parameters are like knobs that are turned to adjust a line to fit the data. A common method is to use linear regression to fit a linear equation to observed data. Whenever you see a line striking through a bunch of data points on a plot there is a good chance it is linear regression at play. In this case, turning one knob adjusts the line's slope making the line more or less steep, while turning another knob repositions the line vertically. Getting the right slope and intercept means getting the best possible fit to the data. In other words, finding the best positions of our knobs is how one attempts to model the relationship between input (independent variable) and output (dependent variable) using data.

Linear regression is essentially a "plug and play" approach, whereby the data collected in an experiment are plugged into a closed form (clean and understandable) expression to produce the slope and intercept needed to fit the line. This means that parameters are not so much found as they are calculated directly.

Linear regression is not *learning* in any proper sense of that word. Linear regression computes its parameter values according to a predefined mathematical structure. If we really want to learn the knobs that define how a function converts inputs to outputs, then we would not make such drastic assumptions about what a function is supposed to look like. Instead, we would embark on what all true learning requires; trial-and-error. This would involve first taking a random guess at the parameter values, seeing how wrong we are (according to some set of criteria), adjusting the values and trying again. We would keep guessing, assessing and adjusting until our approach converges onto some definition of a *good fit*.

This is what machine learning, the computing approach that undergirds today's AI systems, looks to do. Rather than forcing data into some well-defined structure and calculating parameters directly, it uses large amounts of data and iteration to keep making guesses until it achieves convergence. In deep learning, a model is being fit to data, except instead of a straight line it is something high-dimensional that cannot be visualized by our three-dimensional minds. The function learned by AI is not some simple deterministic mapping between inputs to outputs, it is some monstrous, convoluted, impossibly intricate expression containing billions of parameters.

There are no nice interpretable closed-form expressions in AI. We cannot peel back its layers and expose some causal chain of steps that transform information from inputs to outputs. This is not the realm of plug-and-play math, this is the world of iterative optimization and *soft* decision making, used to learn in a fashion similar to how people learn.

Deep learning thus represents a very different philosophy on how to go about building software. Because AI has no explicit or visible function, we cannot know the internal structures that produce its outputs. There is no designing the guts of an AI machine to produce the outputs we need. All we can do is set in place a high-level process that iteratively attempts to turn a billion knobs until it produces the answers we (usually) expect.

The way today's AI is created is by programming individual artificial neurons, which are interconnected units of code created to mimic the behavior of biological neurons in the human brain. Biological neurons are how our nervous system processes and transmits information via electrical and chemical signals. Each neuron in the brain receives signals from other neurons through structures called dendrites. Neurons integrate these incoming signals into their cell body (soma) and generate an action potential (a brief change in electrical potential) if the combined input exceeds a threshold. Action potentials propagate along axons, which are long projections of a neuron that conduct electrical impulses away from its body. Axons are the primary transmission lines of the nervous system, responsible for carrying signals to other neurons, muscles, etc.

In less jargony terms, this means that the human brain seems to process information, and thus achieve its cognition, by using a massive network of interconnected functional units that each transmit electrical signals dependent on their interaction with neighboring units. This is the architecture that inspires deep learning, where the functional units are artificial neurons, and the transmission of electrical signals is information sent between neurons in the form of numerical values; values that represent the activation levels and strengths of connections.

The parameters of deep learning are not things like slope and intercept, as with our linear regression example. The parameters used in deep learning, called weights and biases, number in the billions, and relate to the strength of the connection between neurons, and the level of flexibility permitted within each neuron. Whereas the parameters in linear regression mean something specific thanks to its neat mathematical form, the parameters in a deep learning model only make sense when considering the network as a whole.

How can parameters be set without having an explicit mathematical expression? How can their values be found if they number in the billions? Deep learning does so by passing large amounts of data through the system, and adjusting the parameter values (initially set to random values) until the entire system produces the outputs we need. This is done using optimization algorithms where the model tries to minimize the difference between the output it predicts and the actual output needed. In facial recognition, the actual output needed is the identity of the face (e.g. Bob) and the predicted output is the best guess at any time (e.g. Bill? Susan?). This means the way deep learning approaches problems is not through deliberate calculation but rather by closing the gap between predicted and actual labels until they mostly agree. While not all forms of deep learning use labels, the fundamental approach is the same; closing some gap between what the model initially thinks and what is.

This is a game of guessing and iteration, not reasoned calculation. This more holistic approach to building machines is fundamentally different from how software and statistics has worked throughout history. In deep learning we admit epistemic uncertainty by *stepping outside the system* of interest and only employing a higher-level process that converges on its own. This is a critical distinction, as it shows us an important truth about how complex systems are created. We cannot fashion complexity by piecing together individual things and connecting it up like an internal combustion engine. While neural network architectures are designed in terms of the number and arrangement of artificial neurons, the process by which the parameters inside the network are found and set are out of our hands.

Deep learning distinguishes between internal and external parameters. The weights and biases are the *internal* parameters that directly affect the model's use and transformation of information. There are also hyperparameters, which are external to the model architecture itself. These can be thought of as settings or configurations that govern the training process. They include things like the learning rate, batch size, number of epochs, and various network architecture choices such as the number of layers and neurons per layer.

It is the hyperparameters that are configured by the engineer, not the internal model parameters, and yet it is the internal model parameters that must be set into some specific configuration for the model to work. This shows just how different AI engineering is from anything humans have built prior. In almost all other cases, humans look to reach into the guts of systems and make deliberate choices about how energy and information will move through the system.

People have a hard time understanding the difference between deterministic and nondeterministic processes. The individual artificial neurons are deterministic pieces of code, since the same inputs and weights will always produce the same output. This makes them inline with traditional, rules-based computer programming. However, when these neurons work together in aggregate, the behavior of the neural network is hardly deterministic, especially during the training phase. This is the critical transition that happens in truly complex objects. There is a profound disconnect between the pieces something is made of, and the properties that define its structure and behavior.

As information passes through multiple layers of artificial neurons, each applying its own piece of nonlinearity, the network learns highly complex and nonlinear mappings from inputs to outputs. Whatever deterministic (rules-based) code is used on the small scale brings about something very different at the larger scale. Such complexity unleashes the signature capacity of complex objects to mirror the natural world in a far deeper and more realistic fashion than anything humans could design on their own.

This is how AI systems show signs of true complexity, and why the approach used to build AI is inline with how nature builds. The buildup of many small deterministic nonlinearities into some aggregate nondeterminism is what we see in nature's wet, slimy and dynamic objects. This is not to say today's AI is on par with nature's solutions, only that it mirrors the structure and behavior of natural complexity, and speaks to what happens when you embrace a from-the-outside approach to building things. This is the only way categorically hard problems can be solved. One must step outside the internal workings of a system and allow it to converge on its own, permitting the internals to settle naturally.

This is why deep learning is thought of as a kind of alchemy. This makes many uncomfortable, especially more traditionally minded engineers. There is an ongoing effort to try to explain AI mathematically, which smacks of the reductionism and determinism that works directly against complexity. I will elaborate on this issue later.

Deep learning models are objects that verge on true complexity, because their functionality relies on properties that were never put into the system by us. In some sense, things like cities, financial markets and AI were not created at all, rather they precipitated out from the countless interactions of smaller things that look nothing like the bigger things they led to.

More important than whether AI systems are truly complex is the fact that AI engineering is our best example of humans building under a completely different paradigm. Deep learning represents the first deliberate attempt by humans to *not* build the way humans always have. While the emergence of electrical grids, cities, markets and the internet were realized later, deep learning embraced a fundamentally different paradigm from the onset. Deep learning is possible because it does not attempt to instruct a computer how to carry out its tasks.

Whether or not today's approach to AI achieves true artificial general intelligence (AGI) is not the point. Deep learning is a sign of things to come. Deep learning represents the kind of engineering that redefines how humans build things. We know that we cannot solve our most outstanding challenges using the deterministic engineering of our ancestors.

This is not just a shift in how we build things. It gets to the very heart of how our world currently defines knowledge, skill and the ability of individuals to contribute to the economy. Our world runs on the notion of design, because design is all about reaching into the guts of systems and using what we see to take the next step. Design maps the efforts of builders onto preexisting structures. This is not how nature builds.

Hitting Reset

The entire edifice of design-based building that undergirds today's economy, and people's ability to contribute to it, requires a massive overhaul. To embrace the nondeterminism needed to create in the age of complexity we need an entirely different approach. This new approach must be rooted in a position that is diametrically opposed to how we currently expect to build things.

There is a fundamental directionality to how complexity works, and it is opposite to what we are told by the academic narrative. It is not foundations that lead to good things, it is intermixing, chaos and uncertainty that bring about the structures we end up codifying in our textbooks. In simpler terms, the groundwork, the structuring, the *design* we are told to put in place from the onset of a project directly works against what is needed for the right structures to emerge.

Hitting reset on how we go about building things, defining a proper notion of merit, and fashioning an economy inline with the needed shift, demands a demystifying of emergence. This requires laying out a conceptually succinct description of what emergence is; one that aligns with known scientific properties of information, computation and evolution.

I have not found such an exposition to exist. Despite ongoing attempts by today's scientists to explain emergence, all fail for the same reason (including those made by many "complexity scientists"). They all attempt to explain emergence within the current scientific paradigm. On one hand this should not be too surprising, after all, how else would one publish papers? But this inevitably leads to the kind of reductionism that runs counter to complexity.

Complexity needs a different kind of explanation, unlike those found in the annals of science and engineering. Not an explanation of causality but of properties. The kind of explanation that does not reach into the guts of systems, wrapping outdated notions of averages and renormalization onto its pieces. Such explanations erroneously suggest that what we observe at the high-level is merely some smeared-out fuzzy version of what we see at the lower level. Such attempts are steeped in outdated notions of root cause and pathways, which unsuccessfully try to coerce complexity into the linearity and determinism of simple systems.

Instead, we can see complexity as the inevitable outgrowth of physical systems that solve their hard problems, by settling into organized configurations on their own. We need not appeal to theories that call together matter by strict cause-and-effect. Nor must we conjure up some ill-defined argument that attempts to stuff our gaps in knowledge with meaningless abstract descriptions. Not having a causal explanation for something does not mean it cannot be explained. Mechanisms can be revealed that adhere to the properties and constraints of natural systems, without concocting fairy tale stories about how pieces bump into pieces.

The first step towards a resolution to the hurdle posed by progress by abstraction in the face of complexity is obvious. Humans have always looked to nature for inspiration. Most things we build have some counterpart found in the natural systems that surround us. It is nature that lets us know what is possible. But using nature as our muse is no longer enough. Nature tells us far more than just what is possible. If we step back, shed our reliance on reductionism and determinism, and accept complexity for what it is, we can also learn *how* nature produces her complex solutions. We can learn to build as nature builds.

Chapter 3

Nature as Builder

True Sophistication

Nature is our best example of solutions being created to solve hard problems. Nature's solutions are the organic and inorganic assemblages of matter that solve a host of naturally difficult challenges. The river solves water distribution, erosion control, nutrient transport, habitat creation and flood regulation. The mountain solves water capture, biodiversity, climate regulation and carbon capture. The beaver solves wood harvesting, dam and lodge construction, food storage, territorial defense and family structuring.

When we look to the sky and see a bird flying, we want to fly ourselves. When we see a dolphin glide through the water, or a duck sitting effortlessly on its surface, we wish to do the same. The human body is ill-equipped to survive in natural environments, compared to most animals. We have no fur to keep us warm, claws to defend ourselves, or sizable teeth to incapacitate prey. But we do have an impressive ability to work together and turn ideas into physical tools.

Our ability to observe and recreate aspects of nature is a core part of what it means to be human. When we inspect the fins of a fish, we intuitively realize the connection between surface area and propulsion. We do not leave such realizations where we found them, rather we take matters into our own hands, fashioning fins for ourselves. Observing the flow of water in a river compels us to build our own version of water distribution and flood regulation. Observing a mountain inspires us to craft high standing structures with streamlined shapes to reduce energy consumption, or to protect us from elements (and people). Our techniques in landscaping and engineering mimic some of the structures and functions of beaver dams. Our clothing and textiles attempt to reproduce the warmth and water-repellent properties of various animals.

Humanity has always looked at nature's solutions as inspiration to craft the things we use to survive. But the things humans create are nowhere near as sophisticated at nature's solutions. Is the automobile faster than a cheetah? Depends how you define *fast*. If we are talking about things in one dimension, as a linear movement on a flat surface then of course, the automobile is faster. But such an environment is highly contrived, invented by humans to account for the gross inability of the automobile to move in most environments. The automobile is useless in virtually all natural settings. We cannot speed through a jungle. Our tires would lose grip in the sands of a desert. Sure, we can change the tires and rig better underlying mechanisms (add more pieces) but it will not move as nature's solutions move.

The cheetah can maneuver around corners, turn on a dime, accelerate rapidly and maintain balance under a variety of changing conditions. The cheetah is far more capable than the automobile in almost every respect. This is true for all human-created things. While they appear sophisticated, they pale in comparison to what nature can create. Only by crafting artificial environments do human-created things look capable. A car needs a road to be considered fast, a plane needs an open sky and a direct route to be considered efficient, a drug needs ignorance of side effects to be called "targeted." Nature's sophistication far surpasses what humans make.

We have added many pieces to our solutions. But bridges, passenger jets and microchips are still fully deterministic. They do not produce their outputs using anything other than rules-based instructions and deliberate engineering. Each piece of our inventions has known interactions and visible causal pathways. The inside of an automobile's internal combustion engine, no matter how advanced and intricate, has well-defined, fully deterministic behavior. Of course, errors can introduce unpredictability, but that is from an outside source. The system itself produces outputs in a fully determined and predictable fashion.

Much of human progress has been more about changing the world to suit our limited ability to build, rather than coming up with astounding levels of innovation. When we take an honest look at the difference between human versus natural creation, we see that humans have not been creating true sophistication. Other than things like cities, markets and

AI, almost none of our solutions have the signature hallmarks of complexity. As such they are not objects that solve truly hard problems. Man's creations are only deemed sophisticated in juxtaposition to the narrowly defined world we have made to suit them.

When people look at a rocket engine, they call it "complex" because they are thinking in terms of what we have built before. There are far more pieces and connections in a modern rocket engine than an ancient gunpowder rocket. But now compare a man-made rocket to a squid's propulsion system. They are both propulsion devices operating through a fluid medium, but the squid has capabilities a rocket engineer could only dream of. Squids have extremely fine control over speed and maneuverability. They can achieve both short bursts of speed and prolonged travel, without rapidly exhausting their energy reserves. The squid's nervous system allows it to sense their environment and adjust their propulsion in real-time. The structures of a squid's propulsion system regenerate and maintain themselves.

The rocket is "better" only in its capacity to do one very narrowly defined thing. The rocket's fuel and components are consumed and degraded during use. Sure, the squid is not flying to the moon, but that is not the problem it evolved for (if it were, it would be far more effective than our rockets).

Looking at nature's solutions, we do not see the same kind of intricacies we do inside human inventions. This is because the countless number of details inside nature's solutions get smoothed out by complexity. The rocket engine is not a complex object, not even close. No matter how many pieces are added to the engine it will never be complex if its inputs (fuel and navigation commands) deterministically map to its outputs (thrust and aerodynamic stability).

True sophistication is required to solve hard problems, but it is a wet and slimy sophistication, not one of detailed intricacy. When things appear intricate, they are in fact simple, since we can *see* the inner workings of the apparatus. Complicated is not complex.

Human-invented things are not examples of true sophistication because they have root causes, along with visible causal paths that produce their outputs. They can be debugged when something goes wrong. We can create fancy diagrams and mathematical formulae for their inner workings. This is not sophistication, this is blatant simplicity. You cannot debug complexity.

How is nature able to create such extreme levels of sophistication? How does nature produce solutions with far more pieces and connections than anything humans can fashion? How does nature bring about the highly adaptive cheetah and the extremely capable squid?

We have already seen what hints at such a process. We saw how cities and AI both produce their configurations via a lack of design. We saw how the hallmarks of complexity can be arrived at in human-made things, as long as we are willing to step outside the system and allow things to converge on their own. It turns out that such an approach is the very thing nature has been doing all along.

Nature's Recipe

True sophistication can only be arrived at using nature's recipe; the ingredients of natural selection. Natural selection is a process with three main parts; variation, iteration and selection. Variation represents the differences that exist among individuals within a population, in terms of their physical and behavioral traits. Iteration is the repeated cycles (generations) of the process through which variations within a population are subjected to environmental stressors. Selection is how certain traits within a population are favored or disadvantaged by its environment, leading to changes in the frequency of those traits over time.

The variation in natural selection comes from a variety of sources. In the context of genetics, variation is attributed to things such as mutation, recombination, gene flow and genetic drift. But differences in habitat, climate, food availability, and other ecological factors can also lead to variations in behavior, morphology, and physiology among populations. Mating systems, social hierarchies, communication methods and various group dynamics can shape behavior and traits. And epigenetic mechanisms, whereby environmental factors are experienced during critical developmental periods, can also have lasting effects. Needless to say, variation comes from many sources.

But having a lot of variety is not enough. There must be many iterations to filter out the variations that do not prove worthwhile; the ones that do not adequately solve the host of challenges related to survival. Iteration in nature is made possible via generations, as successive stages of offspring produced by a population over time. No individual lives forever. This boundary on life ensures that a single organism must produce offspring to continue its lineage.

Variation and iteration work together to ensure there are many options to choose from, and many attempts made. But there is one more critical ingredient to nature's recipe, and that is selection. There must be some qualifier of what "good" means. This comes by way of selection pressures, which are the set of criteria life must comply with in order to survive. If a new generation introduces a change that adheres less well to the environment, then they are less likely to survive, and vice versa.

What is most important about nature's recipe of variation, iteration and selection is that it works from the *outside*. There is no deliberate piecing together of inner details for the solutions nature creates. The guts of what is needed emerge automatically from nature's continual process of iterative change and convergence.

One might argue that DNA goes against this notion of automatic solution making. After all, we often refer to DNA as genetic instructions used in the growth, development, functioning and reproduction of all living organisms. DNA stores the code for assembling proteins, needed for the formation of organic matter necessary for life. But DNA itself is a result of natural selection. It is not some beginning of the process, rather its molecular structure was arrived at because simpler molecules were better at replicating and preserving the information needed to sustain life. DNA emerged over billions of years through a process of chemical evolution. The DNA we see today is just one instant in time of a very long process.

Furthermore, DNA itself is a human demarcation; a convenient definition. This does not mean DNA is not real, it just means we choose to place a great deal of importance on its isolated structure. But that structure means nothing without all the surrounding physical context that makes its role possible. Again, complexity does not have root causes.

Natural selection shows us that operating from the outside is how true sophistication is arrived at. By existing outside any kind of inner knowledge about how things work, natural selection allows the chaos of matter and information to naturally configure itself into what is needed to survive. This is how solutions to hard problems are made.

This is why arguments like *intelligent design* fail. Not just because they are unfalsifiable, but because they begin with the premise that complexity would be designed. Believing complexity would be designed, even by a supernatural being, does not conform to how complexity works in the first place. This is not against a belief in God, it is against the improper framing of complexity; something many scientists are equally guilty of. Nature does not design, and the real reason is that design only works under deterministic settings, for which complexity is not. If there is a God, He would not have designed the universe in the deterministic sense, He would have put in place a high-level, external process that allows nature to converge automatically; an approach far more beautiful.

Nature has always been our muse. We have always looked to nature for inspiration, and attempted to mimic her solutions. But there is a much more important message here. Nature shows us that to produce highly flexible and dynamic solutions, the kind that solve truly hard problems, an external process of variation, iteration and selection is the only way. This is about stepping outside the systems we hope to create. This is about admitting the absolute epistemic barrier to figuring out how something works from within. But even more to the point, it is not a matter of difficulty or obfuscation. The absence of causality (not causal opacity, *absence*) in complex systems is not a matter of degree. It is a stark transition that switches the regime of problem solving.

While natural selection is talked about in the context of biology, it is not relegated to just biology. Natural selection is a universal process by which complexity is achieved and evolved. Regardless of the system, if it is to achieve something beyond the kind of simplistic complication we see in human-made systems, it must leverage massive levels of variation, iteration and selection to converge on things that are truly sophisticated.

Natural selection is nature's version of trial-and-error. Nature does not deduce its way towards its solutions. Deduction alone cannot produce an answer to a hard problem because deduction cannot foresee the trade-offs that occur between features inside a complex space of possibilities. There is no analytical way to assess how the countless features inside a complex situation interact.

The patterns of chaos that begin with the three-body problem make it impossible to know exactly (mathematically, analytically) how a thing functions, and this uncertainty increases exponentially with the number of pieces in the system. The only way to achieve the right configuration of matter is to operate externally to the inner details.

Nature's recipe is not about aligning details into some specific arrangement, it is about landing on arrangements automatically; arrangements that compute the right output because that is what survived. This means that nature, above all, is about computation. Nature creates solutions that compute answers to the hardest problems, and they do so in a way that is entirely unlike human-made machines. In fact, framing nature in terms of computation is a far more intellectually honest way to understand nature, compared to most traditional scientific approaches. It is also a good starting point for demystifying what emergence truly is.

Nature as Computation

Viewing nature through the biological lens is not the only option. We can also see nature through the lens of computation. All systems in nature compute, since there are inputs, outputs and a process in between. The mountain is a structure whose inputs are wind and rain that get computed into outputs like climate regulation and carbon capture. The beaver is a structure whose inputs are predators, food, territory, temperature fluctuations, droughts and parasites. All of these must get transformed into something that leads to outputs that enable a beaver's survival; gnawing, food storage and lodge construction.

This is not some forced analogy. Computation is not something that belongs to man-made machines. We usually think of computing in terms of performing calculations, processing data, or executing algorithms to produce a result. But in reality, computing does not depend on algorithms or logic gates. Computing is the transformation of input information into output information, through one or more operations. An operation is simply an action carried out to achieve an outcome within a system or process. An action need not even be something that moves. An action can be carried out by something that stands completely still, by virtue of its juxtaposition to what moves around it. This relative notion of action means things like mountains and riverbeds also compute. Amidst the flux of activity, both inorganic and organic objects transform matter, energy and information into new things. That is how nature's problems are solved.

This reframes how we think of computation. Ultimately, computing is not about procedures, rules or following a series of steps. It is objectively about the transformation of information. This better, more ultimate definition allows us to recast computation in far more rigorous terms, shedding light on the universal properties that computing brings to nature. The most important of those properties is not about procedures at all, but about abstractions.

In chapter 1 I stated that progress by abstraction is a universal truth. By this I mean any process that might resolve harder problems over time must do so by abstracting inner details into higher-level constructs. This is as true for inanimate objects as it is for human beings and the things we build. It might seem odd to consider a mountain or a beaver as being composed of physical abstractions, but in computational terms, this is precisely what they are. Mountains and beavers are not objects who produce their outputs using sets of deterministic steps. It is not algorithms that convert wind and rain into climate regulation, or territory into lodge construction. Nature's solutions are collections of matter that are arranged through evolution to convert inputs into output, absent simple causal pathways.

This makes physical abstractions the primary computing constructs of complex things. Not logic gates or algorithms; physical abstractions. This is because computing in nature must do what all abstractions do, which is to map many possible inputs down to a few needed outputs. Only physical abstractions can produce what the mountain, the river, the cheetah and the beaver produce.

Mountains, while appearing simple from a distance, are incredibly complex structures with numerous intricate facets and sophisticated features. Tilted, folded and faulted layers are a byproduct of various tectonic forces. Mountains often contain a variety of rock types, representing different geological processes and periods throughout their history. In fact, mountains are not static objects at all, as they are often located at or near tectonic plate boundaries, leading to a host of complex interactions such as subduction, rifting, and continental collision. Mountains are subject to various forms of physical, chemical and biological activity. These break down rock and reshape the mountain and surrounding landscape, leading to a unique structure that solves hard problems.

When we look at nature, we are looking at computation on a massive scale. Not the kind of computation we see in traditional computing, but the kind of computing that only complex objects can perform. Computation that rests its core abilities on the presence of physical abstractions that compress information to solve problems.

Internal vs External Processes

Nature's recipe of variation, iteration and selection is not how nature computes the answers to problems, rather it is how nature *finds* the physical solutions that compute answers to problems. This is the difference between an internal and external process. Natural selection is an external process that is wholly unconcerned with the internals needed to solve a problem. Of course I do not mean unconcerned in the conscious sense, only that nature's recipe remains ultimately disconnected from the details inside the objects it fashions.

An internal process is one that does the actual computation to produce the outputs needed. In most human-made objects the internal computation is set deliberately. This means that for almost all the things we have created throughout human history, discovery is only used to find the pieces that end up getting strung together via design, to make the computation happen. But for complex things, the discovery process is used right up until the point the object functions; when the object becomes usable. Whereas traditional engineering must use design to create its computing constructs (e.g. the interaction between rifle components to compute the firing of a bullet), complexity sees its computational constructs emerge automatically, through discovery alone. With natural selection, by the time the solution is discovered it is already assembled, with all the necessary guts required to compute in the wild. Discovered, not designed.

We saw the same external process used in deep learning. Deep learning is not about engineering the specific inner details to compute outputs, it is programming a scaffold that implements the external process of variation, iteration and selection. A variety of data, millions of iterations and selection against optimization criteria ensure that deep learning is essentially a narrow reconstruction of natural selection. This is why deep learning is able to realize inner computations that were never put there by engineers. Deep learning works thanks to emergent abstractions that compress information, as all truly complex solutions do. Deep learning is possible because of a building approach that steps outside the system it looks to create, allowing things to converge on their own, until the necessary computational constructs arise automatically.

With technologies like deep learning, humans are beginning to see what it means to build things that solve naturally hard problems. But it is not enough to merely appreciate distinct processes that solve different problems. To understand how complexity works, and to demystify what emergence is, we must also understand where the "hard" in *hard problem* comes from.

Chapter 4

The Essence of a Hard Problem

Problem, Process, Answer and Solution

The 4 most important terms related to problem solving are problem, process, answer and solution. The *problem* is the task we are working on; the situation that we hope to resolve. The *process* can either be the method by which the solution is found (external) or the method by which the found solution computes its outputs (internal). The *answer* is some final state of the situation that confirms the problem has been solved. The *solution* is the physical object that implements the internal process used to resolve the problem.

If we are talking about a bridge, the *problem* is ensuring a safe and efficient means for vehicles and pedestrians to cross rivers, valleys or roads. The *external process* is the trial-and-error used to discover the final configuration of pieces, while the *internal process* is the causal connection between bridge components that make the bridge function correctly. The *answer* is seeing vehicles and pedestrians on the other side of the river. The *solution* is the bridge itself; the final configuration of pieces we call a bridge.

If we are talking about a deep learning model, the *problem* might be facial recognition. The *external process* is the training phase used to arrive at a good model. The *internal process* is the computing done by whatever materializes as a model upon convergence (more on this later). The *answer* is the correct name for the recognized face, and the *solution* is the deployed model, with its settled (already discovered) set of parameters (weights and biases), placed into production.

Let us do one more. A Rubik's cube has the *problem* of aligning all six faces so that each face consists of a single color. The *external process* is the trial-and-error (or systematic approach) used to find a set of steps others can follow to solve the cube. The *internal process* occurs when one follows that now-discovered set of steps (the "algorithm") to solve the cube. The *answer* is the final solved state (each face consisting of a single color), and the *solution* is the discovered set of steps used by others to solve the cube (perhaps written on a piece of paper).

In summary, the problem is the situation we need to resolve. The external process is how we find the solution (e.g. deduction or trial-and-error). The internal process is how the found solution gets implemented (e.g. step-by-step or something else). The answer is the final state that confirms resolution, and the solution is the physical object that is deployed to carry out the process used to solve the problem (e.g. rules on a piece of paper, a deployed model in software).

Now that we have the language to discuss problem solving, let us develop a solid intuition for understanding what a hard problem is.

What Makes a Problem Hard?

People call problems "hard" when they are not easy to solve. A predicament that has no immediately available solution is usually considered a hard or difficult situation. But computationally the word hard means something more specific. Something is a computationally hard problem if it is very difficult or practically impossible to solve efficiently with a computer. Such a problem requires a great deal of resources, which means a lot of time and/or memory to compute.

Computationally hard problems see their difficulty increase rapidly as the size of the input grows. This is typically of an exponential nature, whereby a small increase in the size of the problem makes the time needed to solve it explode. Exponential growth can be understood by folding a piece of paper again and again. Each fold does not add just a few more layers, rather it grows in multiples. To put this into perspective, if you folded a piece of paper 42 times it would span the distance between the earth and moon.

The computational version of folding paper is the explosion in possible paths an algorithm might take to find a solution. Recall that hard problems have many factors that must be attended to. The longer bridge has more pieces to account for the additional factors involved in the challenge it solves. Facial recognition is difficult computationally because the number of factors involved in making a face a face is immense.

The concept at the heart of what makes problems computationally hard is the *possibility space*. The possibility space is the set of all possible combinations, arrangements, or states that could exist relevant to the problem at hand. This is the set of all possible configurations a system can take on. If we are talking about a chess board, it is all the ways we could arrange the pieces. The larger the possibility space associated with a problem the more space any algorithm that attempts to solve it must traverse. It is this increased level of exploration that is the essence of what makes a problem categorically hard.

Because working within the universe of all possible configurations is infeasible, the possibility space is not where models and algorithms operate. Instead, we must define a reduced set of possible features for a hard problem, and attempt to operate inside that reduced space. This reduced space is called a *feature space*, made of the features we deem important to the problem.

Consider the problem of keeping your hands warm during the winter. Rather than mixing and matching random objects together and wrapping them around our hands, we would consider the attributes that are worthy of consideration. These would be things like thickness, loftiness, level of absorbency and strength. If we were to create a plot of these features, we would have 4 axes. The solution to our problem would live somewhere inside the space carved out by the extent of those

4 axes. This is because the correct combination of materials to make gloves work properly would have the right mix of thickness, loftiness, level of absorbency and strength. Each feature contributes a *dimension* to the feature space, and the combination of all features creates a high-dimensional space where the solution resides. When one talks about a problem being "high-dimensional" this is what is meant; a problem whose feature space contains many dimensions, and whose solution/s reside somewhere inside that space.

What makes a problem categorically hard is the difficulty associated with finding where inside the problem's feature space the solution lives. A feature space for a hard problem is a vast territory, consisting of an entangled patchwork of meandering paths and obstacles. With hard problems, there are no obvious markers telling us where we might find the solution.

There are 3 main sources of difficulty that make the feature spaces of hard problems so challenging to traverse, and their solutions so hard to locate. These are 1) the inherent complexity of the feature space itself, 2) the lack of visible causal connections between the different features and 3) the small number of viable combinations of features (workable solutions) relative to all possible combinations one might make.

The inherent complexity of a feature space arises from the interactions and dependencies between its features. In our keeping-hands-warm problem, a thicker material might provide more insulation but might also reduce dexterity. A material with high absorbency might be good for wicking away moisture but could also become cold when wet. The complexity of the feature space does not necessarily make the feature space bigger, but it does make it more difficult to find a path that leads us to a solution. It is very easy to take a wrong turn inside a complex feature space. Consider the inherent trade-offs, whereby increasing the value of one feature might improve performance in one aspect but degrade it in another. Moving through a complex feature space in search of an answer is robbing Peter to pay Paul, again and again.

In general, as the number of features increases the likelihood that those features are independent decreases. This is why high-dimensional spaces are a hallmark of genuinely complex systems, and the hard problems associated with them. This is also why complexity is not just about a large number of pieces, but critically, the interactions among those pieces.

The second source of problem hardness is the loss of visible causality between features in the feature space. Back to our keeping-hands-warm problem. Here we can easily envision how thickness, loftiness, level of absorbency and strength work together to solve the problem. We can use deduction to move through the feature space and land on a configuration that works. We might first take some animal hide which naturally blocks the cold, and connect it to a piece of animal sinew to bind the material and retain the desired shape. We would easily deduce that filling two layers of hide with animal fiber would serve as better insulation than animal hide alone.

The keeping-hands-warm problem is a relatively simple one, despite having some inherent complexity in its feature space. This shows us that if the number of features is small (lower-dimensional), and the trade-offs between features minimal, that humans can probably locate a solution through mere deduction. The first solution will hardly be the best one, but it will work. Deduction works here because the causal connections between the pieces of our solution are apparent.

But now consider a harder problem. Imagine we must find a solution to the problem of keeping our hands warm while building a snowman. Now there are more constraints to the problem. Not only must we keep our hands warm, but we must also keep them dry, and have enough dexterity to handle snow. These additional constraints on the problem may or may not increase the number of features worth considering, but they will likely introduce additional tradeoffs. This begins to degrade our ability to deduce a solution, as the causal fabric between features is no longer clean cut.

There is an intimate relationship between the inherent complexity of the feature space and the loss of visible causality. The more our features "talk" to each other via interactions the more trade-offs will arise, making it increasingly difficult to find a solution. If we choose a material that keeps us warm and has good dexterity, we might find it gets wet too easily. The moment we find a water-resistant material we lose the dexterity. More constraints aggravate the contradictions, dilemmas, paradoxes and quagmires that make it difficult to find our way towards a viable solution.

The final source of hardness is related to another space called the solution space. The solution space sits within cube feature space (which itself sits inside the possibility space), as a subset of possible configurations that satisfy the criteria or constraints of the problem. In simpler terms, the solution space is the space of all possible configurations that produce a viable solution to the problem.

A large solution space means there are more possible solutions that solve the problem, while a smaller solution space means there are fewer. Problems that have large solution spaces relative to their possibility spaces will take less time to search through, because there is abstractly less space to maneuver around prior to running into a solution. The problems related to keeping our hands warm have large solution spaces, since there are many combinations of material that will solve the problem. Consider that our ancestors likely stumbled upon a decent pair of mittens early on.

Compare this to something like the Rubik's cube. A point inside this feature space would be a unique configuration of 26 "cubies", with each cubie possessing a set of values related to position and orientation. This mix of values is the Rubik's cube version of the blend of thickness, loftiness, level of absorbency and strength from our keep-hands-warm problem. The solution space of the Rubik's cube is the set of all possible algorithms that could produce the same final answer.

It takes a long time to find a solution to the Rubik's cube because of the complexity of its feature space. Note that when

I say *find a solution* this does not mean following some already-discovered algorithm, like cubers do. I am talking about discovering the set of steps for the first time. The Rubik's cube has an inherent complexity to its feature space because its features have trade-offs. When we place one cubie in a given position it can easily ruin one or more previously positioned cubies.

And yet the Rubik's cube is not a categorically hard problem. It is best to think of the Rubik's cube as a problem that begins to show some signs of *hardness*, while still being solvable in a reasonable amount of time. Chess has an even larger and more complex possibility space. Chess gets us closer to a truly hard problem. Of course, neither the Rubik's cube nor chess are *naturally hard problems*. As mentioned in the introduction, naturally hard problems are those presented within natural environments, not the games we create. Naturally hard problems do not fit neatly into the complexity classes of computer science. The possibility spaces in naturally hard problems are effectively infinite in size and complexity. But both Rubik's cube and chess are good ways to see the transition from simpler problems (like keep-hands-warm) to those that approach genuine hardness.

To summarize, there are 3 main aspects of the abstract spaces we use to define problems that lead to hardness: 1) the complexity of the space itself (interdependent features), 2) the degradation of causality between features inside the space and 3) the small size of the solution space relative to the overall space. A categorically hard problem has a high degree of these 3 aspects.

If we look at how much space there is to traverse in hard problems, it seems impossible that we would ever find the answer. The Rubik's cube has over 43 quintillion possible configurations. Chess even more. And yet these are still just games, with reduced dimensionality relative to real world situations. The number of possible configurations in natural settings, ones that are unrestricted by human invention, have levels of complexity that can barely be fathomed. As such, the problems in this space are unlike anything found in games.

And yet humans find solutions to naturally hard problems all the time. How can such massive spaces of possibility be reigned-in and made tractable?

Harder the Problem, Softer the Search

It is important to note that due to the combinatorial explosion that occurs with the Rubik's cube, exhaustive search methods, whereby every possible configuration is attempted (until the correct one is found), are not possible, even using our fastest computers. It would take billions if not trillions of years to calculate all possible configurations in search of a solution.

This is why computers that solve Rubik's cubes *must* employ heuristics and pattern recognition to search through the possibility space more effectively. Heuristics are general rules-of-thumb or shortcuts that allow people, and machines, to solve difficult problems without requiring explicit analysis.

Consider how chess grandmasters use recognizable patterns on the board, such as common openings, to play at their top level. This is not some explicit tallying of chess pieces; this is the rapid recognition of patterns that guide players towards good moves.

Again, the Rubik's cube is not a truly hard problem, but it shows us that as the difficulty of a problem increases, the softer our problem-solving approach must get. Here, *softer* means relying on things like heuristics and pattern recognition rather than some detailed analysis of the parts that makeup a problem. The more difficult the problem, the larger and more complex its possibility space, and that space must be searched. This means the harder the problem, the less analytical we can be about how we go about searching. In the keep-hands-warm problem our search was done easily with a little bit of trial-and-error paired with deduction. The snowman problem required more trial-and-error, since deduction became less useful under degraded causality. The Rubik's cube would require even more trial-and-error to find a new solution. Even if done systematically, the use of heuristics is required. Again, the brute force approach, whereby all possible configurations are attempted until a solution is found, is not feasible.

It stands to reason that naturally hard problems, those we find in real life, can only be solved by the softest approaches. And of course this is what we see. Humans evolved to solve the hardest problems of all using heuristics and pattern recognition, not detailed analysis. The emotional cues and intuitions humans use are our evolved versions of heuristics.

Thus, it is not just human-made computers that compute, as per the original definition of a hard problem. Nature computes. And nature shows us what it takes to solve the hardest problems of all. We must step outside the system, external to the realm of deliberate analysis, and explore vast possibility spaces using trial-and-error, heuristics and pattern recognition.

This is why deep learning is here. Analytical approaches and rules-based computing cannot solve truly hard problems. Deep learning is not about analysis or rules, rather it embraces computational versions of trial-and-error, heuristics and pattern recognition. Deep learning can be applied to the Rubik's cube problem, for the sake of potentially finding novel solutions. This has been done, motivated by the hope that such an application might reveal valuable insights, strategies or innovations related to problem solving in general. Deep learning searches the possibility space much like a human would; softly, externally.

But while the search process used by deep learning is conceptually similar to the one used by humans, the same cannot be said for the solutions found. Humans and traditional computing find a solution that can be presented as an understandable set of instructions for others to follow (i.e. a cuber's algorithm). But deep learning produces something very different. Rather than a visible set of steps, deep learning solutions cannot be seen in this fashion. The solutions produced by deep learning are causally opaque and largely uninterpretable. In short, we do not know what deep learning is doing when its deployed solution solves the cube. The obvious question here is why would the same overall approach between 2 different systems, humans and AI, produce such different solutions?

Chapter 5

A Different Kind of Solution

If You Can See It, It's Wrong

The gloves, snowman and Rubik's cube are problems with increasing levels of difficulty, as per the discussion in chapter 4. Despite their differences they all require the same approach to finding their solutions; a high-level process paired with heuristics to move through a possibility space more effectively. The more difficult the problem, the more searching is required to work through the inherent complexities inside the problem's possibility space.

Recall that a solution is the physical thing that implements the internal process used to resolve a problem. Gloves are a solution because they are physical objects made of causally connected pieces that produce the output needed; warm hands. Rubik's cube solutions (the ones found by people) are sets of rules written down on paper.

But the deep learning solution to the Rubik's cube is entirely different. It is not something that can be written down. Whereas the human solution is interpretable, the deep learning solution is essentially a black box. No matter how much we try to peel back the layers and inspect the arrived-upon model, we cannot decipher what deep learning is doing in any definite terms.

This seems like an odd thing. The human brain is the most complex object we know of, yet it produced a solution that was entirely decipherable. Deep learning approaches true complexity, yet its solutions are opaque and undecipherable. One would assume humans and deep learning would produce solutions that are more similar than unalike.

In fact, deep learning does produce solutions that are more akin to human solutions, but only if the problem being solved is categorically hard. The Rubik's cube is not a categorically hard problem. The Rubik's cube is a puzzle with a fixed, manageable number of states and transitions between them. The Rubik's cube's possibility space is large only in relation to spaces associated with simpler problems.

Since the Rubik's cube is not a categorically hard problem it could have either a simple or complex solution. A simple solution would be the decipherable rules version, while a complex solution would be the indecipherable version that deep learning produces. So why would deep learning produce the complex solution over the simple one?

This is because deep learning uses an external process of variation, iteration and selection to build its models, and as discussed previously, this is the recipe that produces complexity. This process is expected to give a solution close in complexity to the problem it looks to solve. Since the Rubik's cube's possibility space has some inherent complexity, a deep learning solution will naturally tap into that complexity.

This is why the deep learning solution, while being opaque, is the best possible solution in terms of performance. Deep learning solutions can solve the Rubik's cube in under a second; faster than even the world's fastest human speedcuber. This is not about robotic dexterity or undistracted machines. The speed comes about by virtue of superior computation afforded systems that embrace trial-and-error over deliberate analysis and accounting. We see this with human solvers as well. The faster algorithms found by humans rely on more heuristics and pattern recognition than the slower beginner algorithms. Advanced cubers use far more intuition to make their way through the cube, using subtle cues and recurring patterns to anticipate next moves while executing current ones.

Humans are searching for a nice set of rules, no different than accidentally baking your best apple pie and wanting to remember how you got there. But humans only do this because today's paradigm expects us to produce things like explanations, and to teach others how to deterministically accomplish a task. There is no reason to believe an explainable solution would be the most performant. In fact, we should fully expect the opposite, especially as we move away from games, towards real life.

Deep learning taps into the inherent complexity that exists in the Rubik's cube problem. It captures complex patterns and relationships in the data used to represent cube positions, including non-linear relationships that cannot be expressed as simple rules. Deep learning discovers strategies that exploit complexity in ways that are impossible to decipher after the fact. This is what the human brain does when facing real-world challenges. We could throw a spear at an opponent on the battlefield, hitting them perfectly, but be unable to explain how we did it. Should we attempt to decompose spear-throwing into a technique, with isolated movements that add together, we should expect a brutally inferior approach to throwing spears.

Deep learning is encoding a kind of *implicit knowledge* within its learned parameters. Implicit knowledge will always be superior in complex settings because it is latent. Latent things materialize out, they are not pieced together deliberately. This truth is so fundamental that explainability itself should be considered a hallmark of an overly simplistic framing of the real world.

Solving truly hard problems demands genuinely complex solutions. What we build in the age of complexity cannot be some simplistic (i.e. complicated) assemblage of well-thought-out pieces and interactions. Whatever internal process is used by our inventions, we should fully expect its indecipherability. Explanations that seek to define how complex things function internally are fairy tales, and can only limit our innovations.

Nature Is Not an Approximation

The kind of approaches used to solve hard problems have always been considered approximations. Approximation occurs when the process used to arrive at an answer is not as good or exact as it would be, had we approached the problem directly. Deep learning relies on heuristics and mathematical optimization to land on its solutions. As stated previously, such methods are softer versions of the more direct, rules-based approaches used in traditional computing. We are told that softer forms of computing and reasoning are more approximate. That what is found through approximation should be considered suboptimal.

This applies to both humans and machines. On the human side, heuristics rely on our personal judgments and intuitions, which introduce bias, "error" and variability into the decision-making process. Different individuals may apply heuristics differently, and this can lead to varied outcomes given the same situation. Heuristics prioritize speed over accuracy. They aim to quickly find a solution that is good enough, rather than spending the time and resources to find what is best. The machine version of this is essentially the same. The use of heuristics appears as a kind of skipping-over-the-essentials that gets us a solution more quickly.

Thinking of softer approaches as approximations reflects what I believe to be one of the core fallacies within the current scientific and engineering paradigm. The only way one would consider the use of heuristics as an approximation is if they believed the best way to solve a problem was deterministically. That only by reaching into the system's details, and seeing exactly how individual pieces work together to produce the outcome, are we being rigorous in our approach.

This applies to both the discovery and application of a solution. Finding a solution using deductive, rules-based reasoning is deemed more meticulous and exacting than jumping around a space of possibilities, banking decisions on high-level patterns. And deploying a tidy, rules-based system seems more rational and prudent than some opaque model whose internal methods cannot be deciphered.

But that is not how complexity works. Complexity is not some supercharged version of what we see in simple systems. Complexity is indecipherable, not because there are too many details and rules to see clearly, but because the mechanism by which complex systems process matter and information is entirely different. The statistical smearing seen in complex systems is not a fuzzy version of the discrete, rather is it the very thing that manifests to solve the problem. Attempting to peer in and find small pieces that work in a deterministic fashion is to look for something that is not there. Yes, there are small pieces. And yes, they interact. But not as some linear chain of cause-and-effect. The interactions within complex systems manifest constructs that do not exist at the smaller scales.

Nature's solutions are not approximate solutions to hard problems, they are *exactly* what computes the answer needed. Nature is not the reduced isolated pieces we use to define current knowledge. Just because we can inspect a molecule and define its constituent atoms does not mean a molecule's structure and behavior can be explained using atoms. Just because the cell has organelles that appear to take on specific roles does not mean we can (correctly) explain cell function using organelles.

Nature's computational constructs emerge as their own thing, across all the scales a solution exists at. It is difficult for humans to envision processing as anything other than a series of mechanical operations performed in order to change inputs to outputs. But processing just means matter and/or information are being transformed, not that it must occur via mechanical or causal means.

Flexible Determinism

In chapter 1 we looked at the difference between deterministic and nondeterministic processes. Deterministic processes are those where the outcome is predictable, such that the same inputs always produce the same outputs. Nondeterministic processes are those where the outcome is not entirely predictable, such that the same inputs can produce different results each time. Deterministic processes disallow randomness within their normal operation, while nondeterministic processes leverage it.

But things are not as cut and dry when it comes to nature's solutions. Nature's solutions have both determinism and nondeterminism. Nature's solutions have what I call *flexible determinism.* Things are flexibly deterministic when they have both reproducible and non-reproducible behavior. Consider the beaver. There is obviously a good deal of reproducibility to this organism, since we always know a beaver when we see one. A beaver has a well-defined look and set of behaviors. The beaver does not produce entirely different outputs for its inputs.

But the beaver is also highly nondeterministic. It must be, since its host of challenges could never be resolved using strict determinism. Imagine attempting to convert the inputs of predators, food, territory, temperature fluctuations, droughts and parasites using some rule engine that always does the same thing. Predators can approach from countless angles, temperature fluctuations are highly unpredictable and parasites can infect at any given time. A deterministic system could never account for the plurality of factors across a near infinite number of possible scenarios.

And yet, the beaver survives. Despite the convolution of arbitrary, incidental, irregular and unplanned inputs the beaver reliably converts the same few outputs each time. This kind of many-to-few transformations are only possible through abstraction. The structures in the mountain, the riverbed and the beaver work because they are physical abstractions that abbreviate matter, energy and information into a few reliable outputs; as abstractions do. Physical abstractions are the core construct of nature's computation because this is the only way its characteristic flexible determinism can be achieved.

Facial recognition is accomplished by humans, not through some detailed analysis and rote proceduring, but by detecting high-level invariant patterns that are robust to changing angles and lighting. If the person we are looking at moves their head, has shadows cast on their face or is drenched in rain we can still recognize them. This is abstraction in action. The essence of a face cannot be articulated using analysis or verbose descriptions because there are no exact deterministic mechanisms that can identify faces. Only by the mind anchoring on something far more abstract can the problem of facial recognition be solved.

To be able to notice high-level patterns, such as a face, there must exist a formidable level of information compression. Details like the distance between eyes, width of the nose, etc. all must be compressed into a very few high-level signals the mind can use to assign someone's identity. This is exactly what abstraction is. The compression of information into few anchors that can be acted on.

All problems in nature are hard. They are not situations that are resolved by slow analysis. Hard problems are solved quickly because they rely on high-level abstractions in the form of heuristics and pattern recognition. A problem that takes a long time to solve is in fact a simple one. This sounds counter to the way we use the term "hard" in everyday parlance, but in computational terms this is true. Only simple problems can be picked apart and analyzed in the reductionist sense. Truly hard problems are not resolvable by such means. Hard problems require high-level constructs to resolve. Only by abstracting away the inner details into higher order things can hard problems be managed. To be clear, we are not talking about finding a solution for the first time. Here, we are talking about the implementation of the already-found solution (e.g. a deployed model or human brain identifying faces). Finding the solution to a hard problem takes a long time, but implementing the found solution does not.

We do have human-made examples of flexible determinism. The solutions produced by deep learning models are reliable enough to be considered effectively deterministic, yet flexible enough to solve hard problems when implemented. This is not about the difference between the training phase and deployed phases of deep learning, this is just about the deployed *solution*. The kind of determinism seen in operationalized deep learning models has nothing in common with the determinism of traditional engineering. Traditional engineering produces solutions whose outputs are fully predictable. While errors and uncontrollable environmental factors can mitigate pure predictability, the internal functioning of simple systems are engineered to be fully deterministic machines.

But deep learning is *flexible in its static form*. The configuration of parameters that convert inputs to outputs are set in place, yet they bring extreme flexibility by mapping lots of information into much less information. This is the kind of determinism found in nature; the kind that is not achieved by the behavior of rules.

Rules can still be involved at the lower level. Ants and termites have local interaction rules that dictate how they interact. But critically, there is no direct line from these interactions to the behavior that emerges. The local interaction rules merely set in place the interdependence leveraged by complex systems. They are not what leads to the outputs that solve the higher-level problem. It is not the rules that are converting inputs to outputs; that transformation is happening at the higher level of physical abstraction.

This is why any attempt to explicitly explain the inner workings of deep learning models is entirely irrational. The mechanism by which deep learning computes cannot be explained in the internal, causal sense. Yet this truth is lost on many scientists and engineers. There is no lack of researchers attempting to give a more "scientific" explanation of what deep learning models are doing. Their misplaced concreteness stems from our reductionist scientific and engineering paradigm. If a description is ever provided about how deep learning works internally it could only be because 1) it is false or 2) deep learning is not in fact complex. All signs point to #1 being the case.

Deep learning systems will never be designed in the deterministic sense because whatever level of determinism they harbor was not placed there explicitly. There is no path from input to output in deep learning, because what a deep learning model manifests is an emergent mechanism that transforms information in ways rules cannot.

Of course, this is not just deep learning. Deep learning is the human-made version of what we see in nature. This is not to say deep learning is as capable as nature, only that it shows us hints of the kind of complexity required to achieve the flexible determinism seen in nature's solutions. The human brain is of course the best example of all. The human brain is the most complex object we know of, given its number of neurons, connections and emergent properties. The human brain is an object with extreme flexible determinism, enabling us to maneuver through our environmental complexity with great generality.

Many scientists and engineers talk as though the uncertainty that arises in complex systems are due to things like external disturbances, noise, or inherent randomness in the system dynamics. This is true for deterministic systems, but not for complex ones. Again, complexity is not a messy version of determinism, rather it operates in a fundamentally different way. There is an abrupt transition when a system moves from simple to complex. We will see what is happening during this transition in Part 2.

We Need to Engineer Emergence

We can no longer engineer solutions the same way we have throughout our history. The outputs that are needed must be arrived at via emergence, and only complex objects can achieve emergence. We cannot make specific choices about pieces and connections that produce known outcomes, rather we must step outside the internals of the systems we create, as nature does.

Building in the age of complexity demands our processes share deep similarities to natural selection, whereby variation, iteration and selection are the primary concerns, while the internal configurations of our solutions emerge on their own.

To build technology is to solve problems with tangible things. This has always depended on design, in order to craft the next level of physical abstraction. But the number of pieces and interactions that must now be inside the things we build eradicate the notion of design altogether. The parameters within the guts of our creations cannot be set explicitly. There is no access to the kind of internal information required to set those specifics, and even if there was, this is not how nature functions. Approaches based on design are rooted in reductionist thinking, and there can be no reductionist philosophy that leads to viable creations that work under complexity.

But building things still requires knowledge about the principles, materials and processes involved in construction. Different things behave in different ways under various conditions, and this kind of knowledge is required to make rational decisions about how to proceed. As with traditional engineering, building complex things that work still demands an appreciation of how structural integrity, safety, functionality and efficiency play out, in the environments we place the things we create.

The difference now is that such knowledge cannot be based on the internal details of our creations. This flies in the face of how science and engineering operate today. To construct an office tower with structural integrity means using knowledge of how loads are distributed within the building. The causal interactions between specific structural components such as beams, columns and foundations are used to design and craft a viable structure.

Creating objects that meet safety standards means understanding how various elements within structures interact, and how they might fail in different situations. To foresee potential hazards and mitigate risks one must make conscious decisions regarding which pieces to use and how to connect them. Consider fire-rated walls, sprinkler systems and evacuation routes inside today's buildings. Our creations have been made efficient by optimizing the internal workings of the structures we fashion. To identify areas for improvement we had to reason about the causal connections between pieces and use that knowledge to streamline processes, minimize waste and reduce cost. When it comes to our creations performing as intended, such functionality has always been possible by understanding the internal mechanisms and processes by which outputs are produced.

All these examples are based on internal knowledge of how things work. As we move into the age of complexity, we cannot merely toss away knowledge about the principles, materials and processes. The difference is we must now reframe such knowledge in terms of external properties regarding the materials and processes that make things work. Just as natural selection arrives at true sophistication using no reliance on internal knowledge, so too must we step outside the systems we create and place our standards there.

To do this we must ensure we understand what emergence is. Not using some reductionist piecemeal story that attempts to connect small and large scales via causal connections, but by using knowledge of the universal properties of information, computation and evolution.

Only by stepping back and looking at what nature is doing to achieve its emergent structures and behaviors can we understand how nature computes. This is not something found within the annals of science. Not because others have not tried, but because their attempts still smack of the old reductionism that thwarts intellectually honest attempts at understanding complexity. What is needed is an objective look at what nature is doing with information, computing and evolution to create her solutions. Only by stepping outside the current paradigm and seeing nature for what it is can we shed our outdated reductionist lens, and bring forth undeniable truths regarding how nature works.

PART 2
DEMYSTIFYING EMERGENCE

Chapter 6

Emergence as Abstraction

The Physical and Informational

To demystify emergence, we need to connect the physical realm to the informational realm. Nature is composed of physical things, and those things solve problems by processing information. Only by connecting the physical to the informational can we gain understanding into what all those smaller pieces are doing when they manifest into bigger pieces.

As much as current science gets complexity wrong, it does offer a few important frameworks, whose concepts are worth calling upon. These are information theory, theory of computation and evolution. I have already touched on these topics at a high-level to elucidate the notions of physical abstraction, nature's approach to building and what it means to solve naturally hard problems. We now begin to think about these areas deeply, to put forward a mechanism by which emergence happens.

This account of emergence is not a testament to any current consensus or agreed-upon description, since none exists. As mentioned, the scientific community is still far too steeped in reductionism to make much headway in terms of defining how emergence occurs. Here I put forward what I believe to be the most rational explanation based on properties related to information, computation and evolution. Although this thesis will undoubtedly share qualities with existing theories, I present it here on its own account.

Let us begin with the conceptual underpinnings of information theory. Information theory is formally defined as a branch of applied mathematics and computer science dealing with quantifying information, particularly with regards to communication. The main tenets of information theory come to us from computer scientist and mathematician Claude Shannon, who laid the groundwork in the 1940s. The core concept we get from information theory is entropy, which has its roots in thermodynamics, thanks largely to physicists Rudolf Clausius and Ludwig Boltzmann.

The entropy of thermodynamics pertains to the microscopic behavior of molecules and the tendency of systems to evolve towards equilibrium, whereas Shannon's version of entropy relates to the amount of information needed to describe or predict the outcomes of a random process. These are usually treated at separate interpretations, but as we will see, they are fundamentally connected. I would take this further and say they are not merely connected, they are in fact the same thing; just seen at different angles. Information always comes from some physical substrate. Both the physical and informational versions of entropy are core to how nature pushes its creativity forward. In short, there was no chance that Shannon (information) and Boltzmann (physical) would not land on the same concept.

Information theory abstracts away from the underlying physicality of the system of interest, which allows this framework to focus on higher-level patterns that emerge from statistical behavior. In this way we can discuss complex systems without getting lost in the weeds of unnecessary (and usually incorrect) details. Information theory naturally moves across diverse domains such as communication systems, biological networks and social interactions, which is important (and unsurprising) since only fundamentally true aspects of nature have deep universal connections to many things.

Entropy allows us to quantify uncertainty because it serves as a measure of the disorder present in a system. Many scientists dislike the term "disorder" when used to describe entropy, as there are cases where systems seem to have more order despite having larger entropy values. This has more to do with semantics than anything. All that matters is that more entropy will mean more uncertainty, analogous to how a more disordered room will be less certain than an ordered one.

In the physical realm, entropy tells us the number of microscopic configurations or arrangements of particles that correspond to a given macroscopic state. It is a way to count the number of possible microscopic configurations that are consistent with the macroscopic properties we observe. For example, things like temperature, pressure and volume (things we can measure) are *macroscopic* properties of a system, whereas things like individual particles (atoms, molecules) form the *microscopic* perspective.

If a system has more possible configurations, it is less predictable, since having more possibilities means having less certainty around what something is or could become. A gas that fills an entire container evenly has higher entropy than if that gas were confined to one side.

Entropy can be thought of as the average amount of information needed to describe or predict the outcomes of a process. If we flip a fair coin, we are showcasing a process with maximum entropy since there is maximum uncertainty around which side will turn up. But if we take a pair of pliers and bend the coin, we will have much more certainty around the outcome, thus lower entropy.

Shannon entropy captures this uncertainty by measuring the distribution of probabilities associated with different outcomes. This is akin to flipping thousands of coins and taking note of how often they turn up heads and how often they turn up tails, then drawing these outcomes as a bar chart, with each bar representing the count of heads or tails.

Of course, 2 bars on a plot are not much of a distribution. Reality is not like coin flips. Real systems have countless possible configurations (a "trillion-sided coin"), and thus any attempt to represent the relative frequencies of those configurations would be smoothed out and appear as a curve. This is what gives the smooth distributions we usually encounter in textbooks, the most famous one being the bell curve. Whereas coin flips cannot produce a bell curve (since there are only 2 possible outcomes) things like the heights of people can. The most likely outcome is the peak of the distribution, since most people fall into that tight range of heights.

But the bell curve cannot capture complexity because it is devoid of interactions. Individual heights are independent. Heights do not "talk" to each other. Your best friend's height cannot influence yours, thus there is a well-defined average height for humans. This is nothing like complexity, since complexity is defined by many pieces with many interactions. It is the countless interactions inside complex systems that lead to the properties that dictate their structures and behaviors, and make the entire notion of distributions far too simplistic. Whatever "distribution" exists in nature, it is unlikely to look like anything we see in textbooks.

The core concept that entropy gives us, which I will use as part of the foundation for discussing emergence, is the notion of many different configurations pertaining to a singular macroscopic observable. That, I will argue, is the key mechanism that best describes the actual process by which emergence happens. Not one of discrete steps adding together to produce the outcome, but one that arises from the most statistically likely configuration.

Most Likely Configurations

Complexity is using physical matter to do things informationally. That is why processes exist in natural systems; to arrange matter so as to convert inputs into outputs to solve problems. Entropy is a measure of information content and thus it plays a critical role in how information gets processed. Since all physical processes transform information, we can expect nature's problem solving to showcase changes in entropy.

Entropy increases when heat flows from hot objects to colder objects, as thermal energy becomes more evenly distributed among particles. Entropy increases when reactants transform into products during chemical reactions. Phase transitions, such as the melting of ice into water, sees entropy increase due to water molecules becoming more disordered in the liquid phase. Any time gasses expand into larger volumes the entropy increases.

We also see entropy decrease (locally) as nature fashions her objects. Living organisms are lower entropy constructs relative to the disorder that created them. Life can organize and maintain low entropy structures thanks to the continuous incoming energy from their surroundings. The arrangement of atoms or molecules often become more ordered when substances solidify from solution. Order can spontaneously emerge in flocks of birds or schools of fish.

We know that entities have higher entropy if there are more microscopic configurations (microstates) that are consistent with the macroscopic property we observe, such as a system's pressure or volume. Imagine you walk up to a system and measure its pressure. That pressure will be the one that has the most microscopic configurations (arrangement of atoms) that would produce that pressure. All the other possible pressures we might have observed can be expected to have less microscopic configurations associated with their values. In other words, what we observe is the most probable state of the system, which, by definition, is the state with the highest number of underlying microstates that produce the thing we are looking at.

Systems naturally evolve towards states with the greatest number of accessible microstates. This is not just for pressures and temperatures. The physical structures and behaviors we observe can be expected to arise because they have the greatest number of microstates consistent with their appearance. This is a general property of how complex systems work, and thus it is not relegated solely to atomic configurations. This is a mechanism that plays out across all scales.

Consider the emergent structures seen in nature. These are patterns that arise from the interactions of many pieces. These pieces are the lower-level microstates that map to some macroscopic emergent structure. Again, *microscopic* does not need to refer to things that are actually microscopic in size, just a level below the one we observe.

The role of entropy in life has long been debated. On one hand, the second law of thermodynamics tells us entropy always increases in isolated systems, implying that structures should evolve towards states of higher disorder. And yet living organisms are in some sense highly ordered structures, characterized by low entropy. The resolution to this paradox is that life's systems only decrease their entropy locally, at the expense of increasing entropy in their surroundings. This means living organisms are not isolated systems, since they exchange energy and matter with their environment.

But characterizing living organisms as highly ordered and open cannot be the whole story. Within a single entity we see that more disorder in the lower levels (higher entropy) should be expected to produce more order at the higher levels. This is why emergent structures arise from the most possible entropy a stable system can have. This means entropy is neither being lowered or increased in any definite sense, rather it is always in flux, with low-level entropy increase fueling the entropy decrease at higher scales.

In any case, the most critical point here is that an explanation of emergence does not require some chain-of-causality between levels. Emergence does not need an approximation based on reductionism or deterministic reasoning. When viewed in terms of entropy, emergence is simply the physical consequence of having the most lower-level pieces of matter correspond to the structures and behaviors we observe, measure and experience.

The stripes of the zebrafish are what we see. Asking *how* they form is the wrong question. No amount of cell-imaging or genetic tools that attempt to piece together some causal story is ever going to answer this correctly. But what we *know* is that the stripes exist at the highest level (n) while they must have arisen from the cells below (n-1). This means the cells below must be existing with the most possible configurations that are consistent with the stripes we see. Of all possible cell configurations, the ones that work to produce stripes are the most numerous.

The ant colony showcases sophisticated self-organization, division of labor, robustness, adaptability and a great deal of efficiency. These characteristics arise as emergent patterns. There is no causal chain that can tell us where such patterns come from, but we do know that such patterns (n) must arise from the most microscopic configurations that are consistent with the macroscopic patterns we observe. This, I argue, is what emergence *is*.

As already mentioned, another important consequence of all this is that entropy cannot be adequately discussed at only one scale. We should expect the increase *and* decrease of entropy to coincide within a single entity. A natural solution will have the lower levels of its system with more entropy than its higher levels. The stripes of a Zebrafish must have a lower entropy than their next level down structures, such as cells. This is why we consider the inner details to be messier than the higher-level order we observe.

This is as true for philosophy as it is for the physical systems in nature. That last sentence would make most scientists cringe, but the source of their discontent is not a lack of objective truth, it is their reliance on a dying reductionist paradigm. Reality is ultimately informational and computational, and within this setting there are degrees of tractability. The invariant truths that exist (have stood the test of time) are the ones that exist at the highest levels of abstraction, whereas the specific details are always in flux.

This is not a value statement regarding philosophy, or some attempt to incorporate them into the discipline of science, this is simply the undeniable logic of how systems behave based on information and computation. This is how (using a proper definition of *how*) nature works, like it or not.

Just as the peak of a bell curve tells us the most likely height we will observe in a group of people, the peak of any distribution is where the probability is most concentrated. It is this highest point of probability density that tells us what we can expect to see. This is where the most numerous microstates of a system correspond to what we observe. Of course, nature does not use anything as basic as a bell curve, but the point stands. Peaks in distributions are what we observe probabilistically because that is statistically where the most structure/behavior-producing configurations reside.

We can thus think of emergent structures as the physical versions of the peaks of probability distributions. By collapsing the thermodynamic and information-theoretic interpretations of entropy into a single interpretation we begin to see what emergence actually is.

Multiple Realizability

Entropy shows us the connection between the underlying configurations and the macroscopic attributes we observe. Whatever scale we view in nature, we should expect the observed structure to be the peak of a distribution of possibilities. That peak represents the most possible configurations that produce the same result. This means that whatever feature we are observing in nature, it is the one that can be achieved in the most possible ways.

Consequently, there will always be many ways to compute the right answer to a hard problem. This is because nature's emergent structures are its computing constructs, and these are arrived at by mapping many possible microstates to its existence. This means it is not physically possible for a single *path* to produce an outcome in a complex object.

This fact alone completely precludes the notion of reductionism, and the premise that nature's systems could be internally deterministic. The individual pieces from which anything in nature is composed are, by definition, not deterministically connected to outcomes. There can be no root causes in complex systems, because something that has the most possible ways to be achieved cannot have a root cause. Entropy tells us that rather than a path existing from input to output, what we have is a system that arranges itself in countless ways to produce the same output. This is how nature structures itself, and it is those structures that process information to produce what we see.

Nature's solutions are multiply realizable. What we measure, observe and experience in natural settings are that which can be achieved in the most possible ways.

All of Nature is Emergent

At this point I will make a strong claim: emergence is not some niche phenomenon that we sometimes come across in nature, rather it *is* nature. When we look at any system at any scale, we are not observing some deterministically determined thing. The pieces that makeup what we see do not have specific individual roles, as much as they contribute to a new synergistic entity; something with distinct and independent existence. Emergence is usually thought of as individual elements producing a combined effect greater than the sum of their separate effects. This is true, but the word *greater* is problematic. It suggests that the whole is still causally connected to the individual pieces. I argue that emergence is an abrupt transition from a collection of individual pieces to an entirely new object with distinct functionality. This emergence erases any notion of causality between lower and higher levels.

The distinct functionalities that arise at each scale is a natural consequence of the informational and computational realization of configurations that compute unique outputs. Nature creates what is needed to solve a given problem, and the only way this happens is by the multiply realizable mechanism of entropy. There must exist a mapping from many possible inputs to a few specific outputs. This cannot happen using deterministic causal paths, only by entropically driven information compression.

Atomic structure is not a result of neutrons, protons and electrons working together in some simplistic fashion. We already know this to be the case, as all atoms above hydrogen on the periodic table cannot be solved exactly. Once we enter the 3-body problem, interactions between a system's components preclude making exact deterministic predictions. Such calculations are treated "approximately", but as I argued in chapter 5, nature is not an approximation. The calculations used today assume underlying determinism and attempt to create some softer version of that determinism. But if nature abruptly transitions its various scales as entirely new entities, these calculations are not approximations, they are more akin to near misses. Approximations are answers that are not as good or exact as they would be if we approached the problem directly. When we use approaches like numerical methods, heuristics, mathematical optimization or machine learning we are not in fact finding "approximate solutions", because there is nothing to approximate. These techniques are not sitting above some deeper causal reality.

I argue that there is no such thing, even conceptually, as being more direct in our calculations. Observing things at different scales (e.g. molecule versus atoms, cell versus organelles) is to observe entirely new things altogether. The calculations we use to model complexity are in fact *closer to the real thing*, not something proximal to an underlying reality.

In other words, good models that appear to logically define or even predict a complex phenomenon are becoming something akin to the phenomenon itself.

This is closer to what some call *strong emergence*. Weak emergence suggests that the properties and behaviors that arise from the interactions of simpler components are fully explainable in terms of the underlying rules and interactions of those components. In contrast, strong emergence makes the claim that the structures and behaviors seen in complex phenomena cannot be reduced or explained by the underlying rules and interactions of the system's components. I agree, but I do not relegate complexity to some niche corner of science. Emergence is nature. All of it. And this is not some mere belief, rather it rests on proposed mechanisms aligned to known properties of information, computation and evolution.

The emergence I argue for here means nature is entirely *disconnected* from the reductionist assumptions of our current science and engineering paradigm. While the reductionist view works in certain situations, it is ultimately incorrect. Just as classical mechanics is quite useful, but ultimately wrong. But whereas classical mechanics is still useful, the things we must build in the age of complexity makes reductionism and design utterly void. Reaching into the guts of complex systems and arranging its pieces deliberately can only produce useless or dangerous outcomes.

Rather than thinking of complexity and emergence as that which pertains only to certain phenomena, it is much more intellectually honest to admit that emergence *is* nature. Viewing nature in terms of its universal properties makes this account a truly rigorous one. It does not call upon indemonstrable tales about inner causality. It is based on what we *know* happens.

Information Compression

Flexible determinism makes nature's solutions nothing like the rules-based engineering used throughout human history. And yet nature's solutions share something in common with rules, in that they are converting inputs into outputs. What makes this conversion so different from rules-based engineering is that nature's computation is not some causal chain of one-to-one events. Nature does not produce the same output for the same input. Nature squashes many different inputs into a small set of familiar outputs that solve a given problem. This squashing occurs in the extreme, in that there are countless inputs that get converted into fewer outputs. Of all the different environmental challenges a beaver faces, it always produces the same few beaver outputs. This is the flexible determinism we see in nature.

The solutions in nature cannot be a set of rules that do the conversion. They must be something else. We have already seen that this *something else* is the physical abstractions created by nature. But what are the physical abstractions *doing* that enable nature's solution to harbor their flexible determinism? The answer must be information compression.

Information compression is another core concept from information theory, which refers to the process of reducing the size of data without losing significant information. In communication, this can be thought of as finding ways to represent data in a more efficient way, so that it can be stored or transmitted using fewer bits. This is typically achieved by exploiting redundancies in data, since repetition or predictability can be reconstructed after a message is received.

Imagine we had a string of letters such as "AAAABBBCCDAA". We could send this over-the-wire in a more efficient fashion by reducing its size, representing its repeated patterns more efficiently. We could represent sequences of repeated characters by the character itself followed by the number of times it repeats, encoding our original string of letters as "4A3B2C1D2A". Our message has been "squashed" from 12 characters to 10. Doesn't seem like much, but when there is a lot of data it can make a massive difference. At the receiving end (decompressing) we can simply expand each character followed by the number of times it should be repeated, returning us to the original message. Modern compression algorithms used in today's computers use this approach to store files, photos and other items efficiently.

Information compression is what nature is accomplishing via its emergent structures. This must be the case, since it is the emergent structures in nature's solutions that convert countless possibilities into the few outputs that solve their host of challenges.

This is why nature is so flexible and adaptive. When we think of the ability of a cheetah to maneuver on a dime, and execute its speed in so many situations, we are amazed at its sophistication, relative to something like the automobile. But the reason this amazes us is because we are thinking in terms of simple systems. People will visualize discrete components bumping into each other and wonder how the animal accounts for so many factors.

But when we view things properly, through the lens of information compression, we can understand how the cheetah is able to achieve this level of sophistication. The countless inputs, represented to the cheetah as differences in terrain, obstacles, weather conditions, competition from other prey, etc. are being pared down to the few outputs that allow the cheetah to run effectively. Human-made objects (other than things like AI) cannot do this. Such objects require individual pieces to account for the processing of information explicitly. There are far too many inputs to convert to outputs for such deterministic machines to operate outside highly contrived and narrow environments. Only information compression realized by physical matter can enable nature to do what it does.

The Other Abstraction

The physical abstractions created by nature do what all abstractions do. They compress information down to fewer outputs. But nature's physical abstractions have much more in common with the process of mental abstraction than with the designed physical abstractions of traditional engineering. Whereas traditional engineering reduces the number of levers one must pull by making explicit causal connections between levels, nature's physical abstractions reduce the resources necessary to compute.

The emergent structures and behaviors that we see in nature are best understood in terms of how they process information. And the way they process information is by compressing countless inputs down to fewer outputs. Just as our minds form concepts that act as common nouns for all subordinate concepts, nature produces structures that subordinate physical details adhere to. Just as *dog* is a category for all dog breeds, so are the stripes of a zebrafish a physical "category" for all subordinate tissues or cells that make those stripes possible.

Mentally, creating abstractions is what lowers the cognitive load in maneuvering through complex environments and solving hard problems. By grouping superficially different things into single categories, based on deeper shared structures, we limit the amount of processing power required to compute answers. But this is not just an informational phenomenon. As already discussed, we cannot fully separate the physical from the informational. The physical structures in nature exist to solve problems, and problem solving is an informational thing. There is always the transformation of information from inputs to outputs occurring in nature.

To view nature's solutions at different scales, such as comparing the whole tree to its individual branches and leaves, is to view a system's different interfaces. These interfaces, its physical abstractions, have been created by nature as per progress by abstraction. The tree does not stop at solving the problem its branches solve, it solves harder problems by fashioning the entire tree.

The branches of a tree and the entire tree address different problems, fulfilling different roles within the broader context of the tree's survival and overall ecological function. Branches are used for maximizing photosynthesis and providing structural support. The entire tree solves the harder problem of anchoring itself to the ground through its root system, and extracting water and nutrients from the soil.

The tree is a system of interfaces that exist at different levels of abstraction, not just mentally, but physically. The demarcations we define in nature, such as "tree" and "branches" are the physical abstractions that have been created by nature to compute answers to its survival challenges. These levels go all the way down. From the tree we move down to branches and leaves, then further down to the microscopic cellular level, down even further to the atoms and molecules that make the cells. It does not matter how we choose to demarcate the different levels, each level is solving a problem, meaning it is processing information of a specific kind.

One could argue at this point that I am merely reifying mental abstractions. That the different scales of the tree are nothing but convenient demarcations humans make mentally. Further, by defining roles and levels it might appear as though I am relying on the very reductionism I argue against. This is not the case, since the roles I am identifying lose their meaning once the group ceases to exist. Under reductionism, the organelles in a cell have self-contained definitions. The mitochondria is responsible for producing energy through cellular respiration. This is true, but that role has no meaning outside the cell. If it were not for all the other organelles and the matrix they sit within, there would be no point in producing energy through cellular respiration. This in fact makes the identification of an individual's role far less meaningful than reductionism would suggest. More to the point, if we attempted to design a better solution to cellular respiration, by targeting the mitochondria, we can expect such designs to lead to poor outcomes.

Mental abstractions are not figments of our imagination, they are units of processing. To define different levels in a natural object is to observe the nested structure of challenges that object solves. We will learn more about the nested structure of problems in chapter 7. The point here is that we are not reifying nature into artificial yet convenient constructs. This is about undeniable computation, not reification. This is robust even to the possibility that we are demarcating incorrectly. Regardless of where one chooses to place boundaries, any observed level of nature (n) is solving a problem that is different from the group of pieces below (n - 1) and the group of pieces above (n + 1).

I discussed how the physical abstractions that have been created throughout human history have all been designed, using inner knowledge of causality to connect the (n - 1) level to the (n) level. But in nature no such causal connection exists. Each level is its own entity with distinct functionality solving a distinct problem. And yet physical abstraction is how progress of any kind must occur, as argued in chapter 1. This means that nature is producing its own physical abstractions within the solutions it creates. In fact, physical abstractions are what emergent structures are. Emergent structures are the interfaces created by nature that reduce the number of "levers" the next stage of progress must pull to coordinate underlying details.

Whereas humans are devising such interfaces through design, nature is not using cognition to make choices about what to subsume into what. Again, nature's recipe is a beautifully mindless process. But this raises an obvious question. If no decisions are being made, how can nature form physical abstractions? How does nature choose which pieces to combine into a bundle at one level (n), to serve the next level (n + 1)?

Humans make abstractions by operating from outside the system. One can only notice that all dog breeds belong to the same abstract category *dog* by stepping outside the system of dogs and noticing what they all have in common. All dogs have 4 legs, teeth, a tail, etc. The precise description of what makes a dog a dog will never suffice, because precision cannot capture what happens under complexity. But the human brain can recognize when a species is indeed a dog, and place this into a mental category. This is also the case for the physical abstractions that have been designed throughout history. Humans use their awareness and cognition to spot how different pieces of a system can be bundled together into a single unit. But how does nature "observe" how different pieces have something in common? How can nature "observe" itself to create its physical abstractions?

Nature Making Analogies

Humans create mental and physical abstractions by making analogies. An analogy is a comparison of two things to show their similarities. Making an analogy involves spotting some deeper structure between superficially disparate things, and abstraction is how we do that. Abstraction allows us to isolate the core attributes or features of the source and target domains, such that we can compare them more effectively. By stripping away the details one can focus on the more essential principles or structures that are common to both things being compared. If we compare the solar system to an atom, it is by abstraction that we relate the atomic parts to the celestial parts.

This means that if nature is creating physical abstractions, it must be doing something akin to making analogies. This sounds quite odd, since making analogies is obviously a cognitive activity requiring consciousness. What would it mean for a mindless process like natural selection to bring about analogy making? But when viewed mechanistically we can see that complex systems can indeed take-on the analogy-making apparatus. I mentioned previously that nature must "observe" itself to note how different pieces have something in common. Mechanistically this means the system must be self-referencing.

Just as an analogy binds things together, self-referencing systems can bind inner details by their shared structures. This binding does not require consciousness, only the mindless process of producing invariance due to survival. Consider how natural selection keeps certain things around while tossing out everything else. This can occur because the outputs of natural selection (a given generation) become its inputs (the next generation).

Self-referencing leads to reinforcing and stabilization of certain structures and behaviors that persist amidst the flux of everything else. This is how all pattern formation happens in nature. Self-referencing leads to the stabilization, selection and reinforcement of particular states or structures. We see this manifest in various areas, such as attractors inside weather patterns, fixed points in ecological systems, the periodic behavior of heart beats, energy minimization within chemical reactions, and the formation of stripes on our zebrafish. This is evolution writ large, not just the parts relevant to biology. The same pattern formation mechanism occurs in our cities, financial systems, electrical grids, internet and artificial intelligence systems. It is complexity that brings about the self-referencing mechanism due to feedback loops, and this mechanism is how we get non-random things to appear and remain.

Self-referencing is how nature observes itself. It is how survival becomes *the* mode by which better things are created. By which some things stick around, and others do not. The structures and behaviors that we see in nature are nothing but the parts that persisted, automatically and inevitably through self-referencing.

It is self-referencing that enables nature to bundle the guts of her systems into physical abstractions. It is these physical abstractions that compute the answers to nature's posed challenges, as already described. Self-referencing builds configurations of emergent matter that compute the needed answer in natural systems. This is why the properties of complexity are so automatic and inevitable. Emergent structures and behaviors need no guide or path, just the ability to bind matter by continuous self-referencing.

Which brings us to the method by which nature is able to reference itself. The final piece in our quest to demystify emergence.

Chapter 7

Going Meta

From the Outside

The concept that most succinctly captures what it means to operate from the outside, in a self-referential fashion, is known as *meta*. Something is meta when it *talks about itself*. A common example is metadata, which is data about data. Metadata describes the characteristics of the data, like its content, format and structure. This allows us to validate that individual sources of data adhere to some overall structure. The same idea applies to meta-analysis. In meta-analysis, rather than just looking at a single study, researchers combine the results from multiple studies with the goal of generating a more statistically robust conclusion.

Going meta is the attempt to learn something deeper and more universally true than any one instance of a group can reveal. In the case of meta-analysis, each study has its own set of built-in biases, which alone can only offer a very narrow version of truth. The point of going meta is to learn a deeper truth at the heart of any system, one that is *latent*. Something is latent when it is hidden and unlabeled. Latent structures have no convenient labels or categories we can use to describe them. But they are undeniably there, and any specific instantiation of a system can only be one facet of a deeper latent truth. Only by combining many instances of something can we approach its true nature.

Critically, going meta is the only way an abstraction can be created. Consider how people make mental abstractions. In the last chapter we saw how abstractions are made by spotting similarities between superficially disparate things. Once the deeper similarities are spotted, we can then create some higher level category, either informationally or physically. This feat cannot be accomplished from inside the system. A solely internal view does not allow one to place a system into a category. Only by stepping outside and viewing something from above can similarities be noticed between the internal parts of a system. This is why one must go meta to create abstractions. Abstractions cannot be formed without a self-referential process that can look upon itself and glue different things together.

Again, this is not just for mental abstractions. Physical abstractions also demand a meta-level observation to bundle inner pieces into single units. Humans could not have designed the next level of physical abstraction in our tools without being able to spot similarities from above. The stick shift of the automobile, an interface that exists at a higher level of physical abstraction relative to the inner parts it coordinates, could not have been created unless humans could envision how different internal pieces might work together towards the same goal. One cannot see this holistic structure from inside the system, only from the outside.

To be clear, meta is not another level of abstraction, as many incorrectly suggest. Abstractions alone do not talk about themselves, rather they exist as high-level constructs that subsume subordinate pieces. But the *creation* of an abstraction is a process that exists outside the system it is commenting on. Abstraction is still *inside* the system, meta is *outside* the system. If we bundle several pieces into a single group and expose an interface, this new level of abstraction could only have been formed by stepping outside the system itself.

While going meta to create physical abstractions might make sense as a human activity, how does this relate to the *other abstraction* brought about by nature? I argued previously that progress by abstraction is absolute, meaning any system that evolves to solve harder challenges must create increasing levels of physical abstraction. I also argued that this has been achieved by nature as emergence. Emergent structures are levels of physical abstraction that compress information to solve naturally hard problems. But how is nature *going meta* to create its physical abstractions?

Consider deep learning models. Deep learning works, not because of explicit rules-based engineering, but because something manifests inside these complex models that successfully converts inputs to outputs. These are black box approaches, so whatever manifests inside cannot be understood in any precise analytical fashion. But we do know there is the emergence of different levels of abstraction that help with this conversion.

With facial recognition, deep learning uses increasing levels of abstraction to progressively extract more complex and meaningful features from the input data. The system first extracts low-level features from the input image, such as edges, corners, and textures. It then combines these low-level features to extract more complex patterns in the image, such as the eyes, nose and mouth. The increasing levels of abstraction continue, as the system combines the previous level into more holistic facial characteristics like facial expressions and poses. Eventually the abstractions capture the *essence* of a face.

This is all possible thanks to the self-referencing aspect of deep learning. Self-referencing in AI comes from the way deep learning systems update their internal configurations using previous passes through the network. As the model makes guesses, which have some level of error, it uses this error information to improve its next guess. Again and again, the network makes guesses and updates its configuration based on how close its guesses are to the end goal. To engineer a good model is not to know the guts of how it works, it is to put in place a good framework of self-referencing.

This is why deep learning is a version of going meta. It is a system that uses feedback loops to look upon itself and validate whether things are going well. Going meta is entirely different than trying to set parameters explicitly, or engineer systems using rules. Whatever rules might exist in the final working solution, they were arrived at automatically, not via deliberate programming. This is why a self-referencing approach to building things is so fundamentally different. It admits epistemic humility by stepping outside the internal details and rests its efforts on variation, iteration and selection to converge on the right internals. It is the antithesis of design.

Since the internal parameter values in an AI model are found automatically, deliberate engineering only occurs external to these. Hyperparameters are the choices humans make to set up the deep learning training phase as best possible. This is another problem altogether, which works inside the possibility space of all possible hyperparameter values. This next level up must operate under the same premise of external-only actions. We cannot know how to deliberately set the best hyperparameter values. To find these humans must go meta, trying many different hyperparameter values until good ones are found. We must experiment with different learning rates, batch sizes, number of epochs, and network architectures until the right combination of these produces better outputs. When we go meta we are *learning how to learn*.

The AI version of going meta uses methods like hyperparameter optimization (HPO), meta learning and neural architecture search (NAS). The differences between these are not important for this discussion, only that they are all versions of *stepping outside* the problem space and operating externally in order to find what works.

Just as meta-analysis synthesizes different studies to try and learn something deeper than anything one study can showcase, meta learning in AI tries to find something no single model will have; some latent structure that converts input to outputs in a highly generalized and powerful fashion. Again, this effort places emphasis on *learning how to learn*, rather than learning any one specific thing.

For deep learning systems to perform well, they must manifest abstractions within the guts of their models, and those abstractions cannot be realized without finding ways to continually step outside the system. This is not just for deep learning. This is true for any complex solution we build. It is the act of going meta that leads to abstractions that transform inputs to outputs in a flexibly deterministic fashion. Hard problems cannot be solved without going meta.

Problem Structure: Nature's Patterns as Reflections

Problems have structure. This structure comes from the levels of abstraction that define a given problem. The ultimate problem in nature is survival. Life must attempt to preserve its existence against an onslaught of accident and ordeal. But survival is only the topmost version of all challenges in life. At a level of abstraction lower than survival are food, water and shelter. Going even lower in abstraction we find the activities that attempt to resolve the higher level. To obtain food animals must hunt, forage, scavenge, filter, graze, dig, ambush and for some create tools. To find water, animals migrate, recognize vegetation, take advantage of rainfall and partake in an array of exploratory behaviors. Shelters are either found or created. The burrowing owl makes its home in abandoned burrows dug by other animals, such as squirrels. We can continue to define lower levels of abstraction to the problem of burrowing for shelter. If no abandoned squirrel hole can be found, burrowing owls will use their beaks and talons to dig their own hole, which presents a new, lower-level set of specific challenges. The owl must select sites with loose enough soil, such as sandy or loamy areas, and find ways to excavate tunnels several feet deep to ensure the shelter is safe. And so forth.

All of the challenges presented to life have a structure to them; a kind of hierarchy. This seems to allude to Maslow's so-called Hierarchy of Needs, but here I am talking specifically about levels of abstraction and their relation to nature's computation. We can always decompose a problem into nested levels of abstraction, with lower levels subsuming into the higher-level category of the challenge.

Since all solutions in nature are configurations of matter that solve the problems they are presented with, we can think of nature's solutions as reflections of problem structure. I do not mean this in just an intuitive way, but in the specific patterns that form. The patterns we see in the fern, the starfish and the coral reef take on the inevitable structure that looks like the problem it solves. Of all the patterns we see in nature, such as fractals, spirals, waves, hexagonal packing, tessellations, dendritic branching, etc. we are looking at reflections of problem structure.

Let us be even more literal. If we are looking at the nested fractal of a Romanesco broccoli or the spiraling arrangement of seeds in a sunflower head, we are looking at the way that organism's set of environmental challenges are arranged by abstraction. The environment does not merely ask the sunflower to survive, it asks that deeper levels of challenge are resolved, so that the ultimate high-level goal of survival is realized.

The objects we see in nature are the consequence of overlaps between configurations of matter and problem structure. Imagine drawing a line between the various levels of the Romanesco broccoli and the nested levels of abstraction in the problem this organism solves. This is true for inorganic matter as much as it is for life. Salts, metals, rocks, rivers and mountains are all configurations that attend to the structures inherent in the problems they solve. In this sense nature's solutions are not so distinct from their environment, rather they are part of the holistic overlap between problem and solution.

As I argued previously, defining problems this way is not some reification of mental perception. It is not a fanciful theory that projects mental constructs onto the physical world. If reductionism were valid, this might be the case. But under complexity it is not. I am not laying out a causal set of deterministic steps that tell a story of how matter moves from small pieces to big pieces to produce the patterns we see in nature, I am arguing for the inevitable problem solving nature is accomplishing; one that is fully inline with what we *know* about information, computation and evolution. It is all too reasonable to see the patterns in nature as inevitable reflections of problem structure.

All of this is a testament to the connection between informational and physical abstraction. The structure of problems presents us with an informational version of abstraction, the kind leveraged by our minds to define our world and maneuver through life. The physical structures we see in nature present us with the physical version of those abstractions. For nature to produce its rocks, rivers, mountains, starfish, owls and beavers it must be manifesting physical levels of abstraction that overlap with the informational abstractions that constitute their environments.

Nature Can Reach Higher

Nature is a far more powerful computing engine than anything humans can devise. While our AI systems have aspects of self-referencing and abstraction, nature takes this to the extreme. Before accounting for nature's version of going meta, consider again our attempt to do this with AI technology. As already stated, we cannot set the internal parameters deliberately, so we operate from the outside by setting values related to training. We choose the learning rate, batch size, number of epochs, number of layers, neurons per layer, etc. These do not direct anything inside the model, they only help structure the process used to learn. We can think of these values as the first level of going meta, since they exist outside the guts of the system. Getting the best values should produce the best possible abstractions within.

But what should these values be? This is its own problem, a meta problem. Here, we are less interested in knowing an individual model's best parameters, and more in learning how to learn *any* model's best parameters. As mentioned previously, this meta problem is approached using techniques like hyperparameter optimization (HPO), meta learning and neural architecture search (NAS). While only one of these goes by the title "meta learning", they all attempt to solve the meta problem of finding the best external values possible (within a reasonable amount of time).

One approach is to combine many different models to learn and deploy a single better model called a meta-learner. The idea is that any single model will be too narrow to exhibit generalized intelligence, but many models might learn something more latent, providing a more powerful entity. But there are only so many models we can combine into a group before the challenge becomes intractable. Each model must be trained on data individually, which involves a series of experiments and validation. But the higher-level problem of meta learning must also be done with experiments and validation, to see which *combination* of models works best. This higher problem has its own set of parameter values that must be determined. But why stop there? We could combine different meta learning frameworks into new combinations, which would have their own set of external parameters, to again be experimented with and validated.

The possibility space associated with combining things into bigger and bigger groups explodes into sizes that are beyond astronomical. This calls into question the feasibility of going meta to engineer complex things. Even if we accept the fundamental limitation of design, is not design our only chance of making building efforts feasible? Sure, we might want to embrace massive levels of trial-and-error just to see what works, but running so many experiments has computational demands that seem to make this approach ultimately impossible.

But design cannot cut through the extreme combinatorial explosion of possibilities. Design is based on a fundamentally invalid premise when it comes to complex things, as discussed throughout this book. Design cannot be the answer. But it seems at first glance that operating at the meta level cannot alleviate the computational demands of solving problems internally. Just because we step outside the system does not mean the lower-level problems need not be resolved. This raises a concern. How can going meta be a way to build things?

As always, nature holds the answer. Nature can reach extremely high levels of meta to fashion entire ecosystems. If we use the taxonomic classification system, we can say nature brings together organisms to form species, species to form genera, genera to form families, families to form orders, orders to form classes, classes to form phyla, phyla to form kingdoms and kingdoms to form domains. All of these are different levels of physical abstraction (groups of living organisms) working together to solve a given problem. Each of these are fashioned automatically, by nature's mechanism of self-referencing and abstraction creation.

Nature can *go meta* far more effectively than human engineering. The computational load that nature is wielding is astounding. Nature keeps stepping outside a given level and finding the parameters that work to create the next level.

Of course, nature's computational resources are virtually infinite compared to what humans have at their disposal. Nature has an extreme version of distributed parallel processing, thanks to billions of its processors working simultaneously within a group. While each piece of a natural system (e.g. a cell, a neuron) only performs simple computations, their collective behavior resolves fantastically complex functions. Nature also operates on far grander timescales than human innovation. Evolution takes millions of years to fashion its solutions through natural selection. Nature can explore an utterly enormous possibility space, using massive variation, iteration and selection, all in a highly parallel manner.

There is also a big difference in terms of energy efficiency, with biological systems being incredibly energy efficient relative to anything humans create. The human brain only consumes about 20 watts of power, while modern supercomputers and deep learning systems have energy consumption several orders of magnitude greater. Consider how effective the human brain is at vision, motor control and reasoning compared to AI, despite only consuming 20 watts. Biological efficiency is in its own category.

Biology is also deeply integrated with the physical world. All levels of abstraction operate in direct communication with their environments. The computations that convert inputs to outputs are occurring as physical processes within the system itself, not as proxy models of behavior. It is thus not so surprising that nature can *go meta* far more effectively than humans. Nature has at its disposal the parallelism, time, energy efficiency and deep physical integration to step outside multiple levels of a given system and create its nested emergent abstractions.

So how can humans operate as nature does, without having anywhere near the computational resources she has? How can we fashion truly complex objects that solve as nature solves, if we cannot meet natural computational demands?

One obvious answer is to hack nature where she stands. For example, synthetic biology looks to engineer the genetic material of organisms, such as viruses and bacteria, to have desirable characteristics. This has been done in areas like bioremediation, bioproduction of pharmaceuticals, biofuels, and even changing bacteria to perform simple logic operations for computing, or act as biological actuators inside tiny machines. Synthetic biology bypasses the need to engineer emergence because we are leveraging already-evolved features.

The core problem here is one of misapplication. While there will be some success in hacking nature's existing solutions, the reality is nature evolves the way it does for a reason. That reason cannot be defined in simple reductionist terms. All we can say is that nature's solutions are what they are because that is what survived. A natural object's makeup is a fantastically complex object that solves its host of problems in ways we will never know. Attempting to hijack some piece of a natural solution might bring some narrow benefit, but it will come with all the problems of design under complexity; they are guaranteed to produce unforeseen side-effects that will likely reduce a solution's efficacy in the long run.

As argued in this book, we must engineer emergence ourselves, not merely repurpose nature for problem's she was not meant to solve. Our creations must establish their own complexities, and arrive at their own emergent structures and behaviors, based on the environments we place them in. There are deep internal dependencies that cannot be seen, that enable natural solutions to work effectively. These internals must materialize out as physical abstractions built via automatic self-referencing.

To engineer emergence ourselves we must look to maximize the parallelism, energy efficiency and deep physical integration seen in nature. Under design, this is not possible. Design forces us to make specific detailed decisions that become highly constrained and unnatural versions of the parallelism, energy efficiency and deep physical integration needed.

Consider how the AI researcher or engineer wants to deliberately fashion systems by making explicit decisions around *how* these systems function, perform, and interact with their environments. They want to identify and collect relevant data sources for training and evaluation. They seek to select and design algorithms based on specific computational requirements. They aim to design the neural network architectures, making decisions about layers, activation functions, connections and optimization techniques, all based on design principles, best practices and mathematical theory.

But the truth is, the biggest strides in deep learning progress have not come from specific design choices, they have come from throwing more data and computing power at the problem. In fact, the specific architecture is far less important than the current paradigm would suggest. It is not that specific structures are not important, it is that they do not arise from deliberate reasoning and design as suggested in research articles. The structures that end up working are largely a *byproduct* of more data and more computing power.

This is exactly what one should expect when building complex things. AI research is effective for reasons most AI researchers do not seem to understand. This will sound like an odd statement to many, but we see this pattern frequently. It is easy for people to believe their design choices are responsible for progress, when in fact progress under complexity has much more to do with randomness and happenstance than design. This is in fact a rigorous statement, one that is fully inline with the undeniable properties of how complex systems evolve.

Design under complexity is correctly understood as something that interferes with the creation of good solutions. Design choices rob complex systems of their natural intricacies and opaque dependencies. They interfere with the kind of internal communication between pieces that must occur to materialize what works. Design also limits our ability to explore vast possibility spaces because of the inflexibility design forces into our solutions.

Of course, the design of AI systems is not like the design of traditional engineering. Again, AI is our best example of stepping outside systems and allowing things to converge. But our level of meta is far too close to the guts of our solutions. Whereas nature reaches all the way up to the domain under taxonomic classification, we are still operating just outside the individual organism. If all we wanted was a basic model that predicts narrowly defined things this might be fine. But in the quest to achieve something akin to general intelligence this cannot work. The more sophisticated and powerful our intended solution, the more genuine complexity we must create.

To achieve the kind of parallelism, energy efficiency and deep physical integration needed demands we operate at levels far more meta than the solution we seek. If we want to build a brain, we will not achieve it by trying to architect a brain. While it seems convenient to define human intelligence as something that occurs inside an individual's head, we are a deeply connected social species. There is no intelligence without levels of aggregation that far surpass a single biological neural network. Meta must reach far higher than the organism to make the best organism. Design keeps us too close to the organism.

When we remain too close to the thing we are building, as per design, trial-and-error becomes intractable. This is because the things we attempt to mix and match during experimentation are too defined. But when we shift our focus to the surface, using only the highest-level, most general problem statement, the internals must figure themselves out. This is how complexity works.

The more difficult the problem, the larger and more complex its possibility space, and that space must be searched. In chapter 4 we saw that as the difficulty of a problem increases, the softer our problem solving must get, and the less analytical we can be about how we go about searching.

We can think of heuristics and pattern recognition as tools that allow us to find things inside massive possibility spaces without having to do much searching. But this only works if we apply them to the highest-level signals a complex situation emits. But design forces us to define searching in overly explicit terms. It does not leverage what nature already gives us. Design makes us attempt trial-and-error on low-level constructs that do not in fact have the meaning we assign them. It is not for us to know how things interact, only that interactions will take place as needed if more of the system is forced to survive stressors. Reaching higher in our meta efforts is getting nature to work itself out naturally.

So, how can we operate at the highest level of meta while not running into computational limitations? The answer is to 1) keep problem statements as general as possible (operate at the surface), and 2) create highly flexible internals rather than designing specifics.

We keep problem solving at the surface by only maintaining the highest-level target we can get away with. An example in AI would be defining our problems as *building an entity that holds realistic and useful conversations*. That is all. Today's paradigm tells us to go much deeper, by decomposing a problem into its purpose, target audience, scope of conversation, intent, context, handling of ambiguity, tone and personality. But this deconstruction of a problem is reductionist. We do not know such specifics, only that the entire solution must solve the topmost definition of a problem. Decomposing a problem into specifics is guaranteed to produce inferior engineering under complexity.

For the second point, we create highly flexible internals by not designing specifics. Consider the activation functions used in neural networks. These are to introduce non-linearity into the model. There are several choices we can choose from, each with its own characteristics, advantages and drawbacks. We can choose sigmoid, hyperbolic tangent, rectified linear unit (ReLU), leaky ReLU, parametric ReLU (PReLU), exponential linear unit (ELU), scaled exponential linear unit (SELU), softmax, swish, Gaussian etc. Trying to mix and match these possibilities with all the other variables that could be changed in a neural network is analogous to moving one cubie in a Rubik's cube only to scramble our previous moves. There are just too many possible choices at this level to make trial-and-error feasible.

But now imagine that instead of trying to design the best activation function as an isolated thing, we create something less defined and more flexible. The closest approach we have currently is something called learnable activation functions. These functions include parameters that are adjusted during the training process, allowing the function to change its shape dynamically. Whether or not this approach works is not the point. The key is to not attempt to design the flexibility, but to put in place something that changes its makeup *as part of a whole*. The less defined the thing is in the reductionist sense, the better. Just as mitochondria lose their definition outside a cell, activation functions have a role that cannot adequately be defined outside a network. It is part of a holistic solution whose presence in the group is what matters. It is not for us to know what the activation function should look like. Only that its structure and function should emerge naturally on its own, while we remain concerned only with high-level targets.

To get the best activation functions, network architectures, data preprocessing pipelines, loss functions, optimization algorithms, etc. is not to design them. It is to let them materialize out by only focusing on the topmost level of the problem we are trying to solve. We must reach meta as high as possible by maintaining flexible internals.

It makes many scientists and engineers uncomfortable that progress would best be defined under such a lack of precision.

But this is how complexity works. More data and computing power thrown at highly flexible, ill-defined constructs is how the best possible structures will emerge. One need look no further than nature's approach to building to realize this is true. This is what it will mean to build in the age of complexity, if we do it right.

The Thing we Are After (Meta Structures)

No two snowflakes look the same. Actually, this is only true in the detailed sense. If we zoom in on an individual snowflake we will see a truly unique pattern, marked by its distinct crystallization. As with someone's fingerprint, the detailed structure we see close up belongs only to that specific snowflake. But zoom out enough to see the entire flake and we see something familiar. All snowflakes can be called "snowflakes" because they share a common pattern. This shared pattern is not something we can define explicitly. If we asked seven different artists to draw the essence of a snowflake, their drawings would look similar, but not identical. We all understand what a snowflake looks like, yet that understanding is not given to us by some precise definition. It is a latent structure that we know intuitively.

The essence of something, like the essence of a snowflake, is what we are after when we learn. To know a snowflake is not to know one instance of it, but to observe many instances and create some unlabeled abstraction in our mind that defines it. To learn, is to understand the deep hidden template that many instances of a phenomenon adhere to, but never manifest explicitly.

This is why there are no words to describe what the essence of something is. If one learns how to play piano, swing a golf club or develop theories in quantum mechanics they are tapping into some hidden shared pattern among countless experiences. It is not something that can be decomposed into pieces and taught directly to others. This is why true skill seems more like a feeling than anything describable. If you can explain it precisely, it is either not a real skill or you are not that good at it.

This is also why experience is the only way to achieve true skill. It is not that one must keep seeing the same thing, rather they must keep experiencing many different instances of the same latent thing. Only then will the invariant truths be recognizable, as they are what persist when everything else changes. A piano player must play (or better, compose) many *different* songs for this activity to imprint upon them what it means to play piano. The golfer must take countless swings, each slightly different, to comprehend what makes a good swing.

True learning happens, not by going deep into one version of something, but by exposing oneself to many different aspects of it. It is the unspoken, intuitive and latent structure we are after. It is what survives the mind, yet has no name.

One can predict the general look of a snowflake, but they cannot predict what the next snowflake will look like. This is why details do not matter in nature, at least not in the sense we are usually taught. Details are only there to be in flux, in service to the next level of abstraction. As per multiple realizability, there will *always* be many ways to achieve the same thing. To view details is to view but one transient instantiation of a collection that serves the next level up.

This means that the only way to really describe or explain a snowflake is to talk about it in the meta sense. Only the general, shared properties of all snowflakes represent true knowledge of a snowflake's structure and behavior. Any detailed account will be steeped in reductionism and causal reasoning, having little to do with why a snowflake looks the way it does.

The real structure that defines the snowflake is its *meta structure*. A meta structure is the latent pattern that shows no direct appearance in nature. Meta structures are the hidden templates nature's solutions attempt to become, but never do. Anything we build in the age of complexity will have the existence of a meta structure, since the emergent structures we see in complex objects gravitate towards latent patterns.

In part 3 we will see how knowledge of meta structures acts as true validation when building complex things (in contrast to things like design principles or supposed causes). Meta structures are agnostic to the internal details of complex objects. Meta structures do not intervene on the natural and automatic convergence of matter and information that makes complex things work the way they do. This is why meta structures represent a tractable form of validation under complexity.

All the Way Up, All the Way Down: Group Selection

I mentioned previously how AI engineering, despite being our best example of working externally to the details, is still steeped in design. AI engineers look to deliberately fashion systems by making explicit decisions around how they should function and perform. I then argued against such efforts for reasons discussed in this book. The best structures we can achieve are a byproduct of operating at the surface, with little regard for the internal specifics of what we build. This saves us from enacting an untenable form of trial-and-error, and instead integrates us deeply into the physical realities we hope to model.

I used the example of the activation function having a role that cannot adequately be defined in reductionist terms. It is part of a holistic solution whose presence in the group is all that matters. This means what we are truly after when we build solutions to hard problems is the existence of the best *group* possible. This brings us to the final aspect of demystifying emergence. How does nature always create the best group possible, and how might humans do the same?

Let us first look at how humans form groups under the current paradigm. This is not the group-forming found naturally, like the emergence of societies or social movements, these are groups like sports teams, university students and employees; groups that are hand-picked for some performance-related purpose. These groups are created through explicit selection of individuals. We want skill diversity, so we hire for specific technical expertise and domain knowledge. We define clear roles and responsibilities, such as leadership or technical know-how. We seek certain personalities, work styles and collaborative skills. We want cultural fit among our players, students or employees, and a shared set of values. There are also experience levels, and sometimes geographical and time zone considerations.

All this selection seems to make sense, until we realize it smacks of design. We are assuming we know the roles different people in a group are supposed to play, admitting people into groups based on these criteria. The reader should realize by now this is not a good way to create groups. All we can know is that the best group is needed, not what specific roles will make for the best pieces. As one might imagine, nature does not make such explicit choices regarding roles (despite how reductionist science likes to talk about roles in nature). Nature can select the best group by doing just that, group selection.

Using our taxonomy example from before, we can say a species exists because individual organisms work together to solve the *species problem*, which is to delineate groups of organisms that are reproductively isolated from one another. Perhaps this helps with genetic compatibility and less error-prone reproduction. Perhaps it ensures different species occupy distinct ecological niches to reduce competition over resources. Perhaps it improves diversification, introducing a level of stability and resilience inside ecosystems. Perhaps it is all of these.

We can expect the next level, genus, to bring further ecosystem functioning and dynamics that are necessary for life on earth. Resource partitioning, pollination, seed dispersal and new levels of biodiversity, stability and habitat structuring all operate at this level.

As discussed previously, all problems have a structure of them, and nature manifests what is needed to solve that structure. The nested levels of abstraction that sit beneath the topmost level called *survival* can only be attended to by groups. A group is a collection of pieces that work together to solve a given level inside the structure of a problem.

This means that the *selection* in natural selection must be *group selection*. This has been a controversial issue for many years, as the idea of group selection runs counter to contemporary takes like selfish-gene theory. Selfish-gene theory was proposed by biologist Richard Dawkins in his 1976 book *The Selfish Gene*, which has become a cornerstone of evolutionary biology. Selfish Gene theory suggests that *individual* genes are the primary units of selection in evolution, and they act in their own self-interest to ensure their survival and propagation. This is thus a gene-centered view of evolution, stating that the ultimate goal of genes is to replicate themselves, while organisms are just the means by which genes achieve this goal.

Group selection is a very different perspective. Whereas Selfish Gene theory focuses on the gene as the primary unit of selection, group selection focuses on the evolution of traits that benefit a group, even if they are detrimental to an individual's fitness. In group selection, the selection acts on groups of individuals, favoring traits that benefit the group as a whole.

The problem with Selfish Gene theory is that it does not align to how nature computes. Suggesting that there is a single type of construct that is uniquely selected by nature does not adhere to what we know about information, computation and evolution. From the previous sections, it should now be clear that nature goes meta at all levels, allowing for the creation of the physical abstractions necessary to compress information and compute outputs to naturally hard problems. If evolution only selected at the level of genes, this entire meta process would not work.

I believe Selfish Gene theory is little more than reductionism found in biology. It is tempting to consider genes as having the primary role in evolution, but in reality, a gene is but one piece of a larger group that gets selected on by nature.

At all levels of selection, in any natural process, it is the group that matters. Atoms take on their essential properties because the nucleus and electrons work together as a whole. A molecule's behavior in any chemical reaction is not determined by single electrons, it depends wholly on how all electrons work in combination. We can keep climbing the ladder of complexity and find an ever-larger dependence on group-level properties.

It is not about the individual, it cannot be. The problem solving enacted by nature occurs at all levels, and only the group can solve the next level up. We know that abstraction is, by definition, the subsuming of many different pieces into a single unit, and that single unit solves a new problem. That single unit compresses information so as to map countless inputs down to the few that are needed. The unit of selection in natural selection must be the group.

Consider the difference between a snowbank and a snowflake. Just as organisms solve different problems than species, the individual snowflake solves a different problem than a snowbank. A snowflake solves the problem of providing numerous surfaces and edges for water molecules to adhere to and crystallize upon. The six-sided symmetrical structure of snowflakes maximizes their surface area-to-volume ratio, allowing them to efficiently capture and collect water vapor from the surrounding air. The delicate and often branched structure of snowflakes contributes to their aerodynamic properties, allowing them to float gently through the atmosphere as they fall to the ground. This structure helps ensure that snowflakes can travel long distances without being disrupted or broken apart.

But a snowbank is another level of complexity, formed by the collective action of snowflakes. In a group, snowflakes solve the problem of insulation, by trapping air within the spaces between ice crystals. This helps maintain a stable temperature within the snowbank, reducing heat loss from the ground. Collectively, a group of snowflakes gives off a characteristic white color (which individual snowflakes do not), which plays a crucial role in regulating Earth's climate, by reflecting sunlight back into space, thus helping to cool the planet.

Individual polar bear hairs solve a different problem than the group of hair. Single polar bear hairs are hollow, which by themselves look transparent, but as a group offer insulation and produce a white color. An individual hair is connected to nerve endings, providing the bear with a highly sensitive sense of touch, allowing the bear to detect changes in its environment. Collectively, polar bear hair solves the problem of camouflage, water repellency and buoyancy.

Always selecting for the group is how nature goes meta. This is because to be meta is to consider all subsets of a group at once, and spot which invariant properties they all have in common. Nature is forever hovering above the details and "noticing" how pieces work together to produce what is needed to survive. Nature can select the best group because it selects not for individual pieces, but for groups.

By selecting for the group nature is effectively making "analogies." Nature is finding connections between things, automatically, because only shared pieces represent the material configurations that survive. By seeing emergence as the natural byproduct of nature selecting for the group, we can understand how nature is able to create increasing levels of physical abstractions; all without using design. This hints at how we might do the same.

The list of things we often consider when designing a group are not in and of themselves bad. It makes sense to have diversity, expertise, domain knowledge, leadership, good personalities, collaborative skills, etc. But these must emerge on their own, just as mitochondria emerge in the cell. The group attributes we hope to see are not for us to select, because we have little idea how these relate to each other in the wild. The way we can select for the group is to just add variety. Not a type of variety, just variety. This is a meta property of all systems that evolve effectively. They have a high level of variation, as per nature's recipe. We can thus also say that aiming for iteration is also good. Not a type of iteration, just iteration. And as for selection, we can now see that it is the group that must be selected. We must select from the top, allowing the bottom-up flux of matter and information to manifest what works.

Building Differently

We have now taken the journey to demystify emergence. Emergence is not some edge case phenomenon that is difficult to explain, but rather the inevitable and automatic process that aligns to informational, computational and evolutionary truths.

We can see that nature's patterns, in all their fantastic variety, are levels of physical abstraction created by the meta mechanism of nature, which creates abstractions the only way possible; by bundling inner details into higher level categories that compute answers to naturally hard problems.

Our reductionist paradigm will never be able to explain emergence, because of its reliance on pieces and causality. The inner knowledge that our current paradigm relies on is diametrically opposed to what makes nature work. It is not a story of defined pieces working together in a deterministic fashion, it is one of entropy, information compression and group selection.

Humans, being a part of nature, have implemented their own low-dimensional version of progress by abstraction. But as we solve harder problems our historical approach to technological progress can no longer work. We must now look to nature and her mechanisms to realize how true sophistication is achieved.

This has drastic consequences that go well beyond technological progress. This gets to the heart of how we define knowledge, skill and even quality of life. It strikes at our notions of meritocracy and people's ability to contribute to the economy. We must bring forth a new era of human innovation that eschews the notion of design. There can be no reliance on predetermined structures or inner causal knowledge, because that is, simply, not how nature works.

PART 3
REDEFINING KNOWLEDGE

Chapter 8

Properties over Reasons

Invariance as Truth

Knowledge is the information and understanding that enables individuals to comprehend and interpret the world around them. The pursuit of knowledge must align to the pursuit of truth, otherwise it is not knowledge, it is agenda. We can say that truth is something that persists, relative to many other pieces of information.

This means that truth aligns to the notion of abstraction. This is because an abstraction is a higher-level category with subordinate concepts, and only the category is robust to changes. Imagine half of all dog breeds vanished. This would do nothing to the category *dog*. The same can be said if 1000 new dog breeds came onto the scene. As long as there exists a collection of conceptually related details, the higher-level construct will persist. Abstractions survive much longer than the details that fall into them.

The reader should now realize that the same is true for physical abstractions. The configurations of matter that exist at higher levels always outlast the inner details at lower levels. Remember, this is for complex systems, not simple ones. If we remove a gear from inside of the transmission of a car (simple system) then the stick shift will cease to function. But in a complex system this is not the case. The high-level physical abstraction is a consequence of many configurations that map to the "stick shift" of the system. This is due to the entropic consequence of multiple realizability, as we saw earlier.

The emergent structures and behaviors that we observe have the most possible ways to be achieved. This is why they are invariant. If the things we observed were made possible thanks to just a few well-defined pathways, they would be far too fragile to survive the vagaries of natural environments.

This means that the higher the level of abstraction we are observing, the more invariant it is. This is, again, true for both physical and informational versions of abstraction. This shows us that we have an anchor for discerning whether something is more likely to be true. Just as nature only preserves that which can survive, truth is that which remains invariant despite the flux of everything else. Hence the title of this section; invariance as truth.

The knowledge that we are after, which must be aligned to the notion of truth, cannot be based on the inner details. Inner details are by definition transient, and thus cannot tell the story of what is. But the most abstract, high-level patterns that emerge have far more permanence, and thus speak to things that are true about nature and life in general.

This brings us to a critical realization about our concept of knowledge. The idea that knowledge is something we keep accumulating does not make sense under complexity. Knowledge must be something that *converges*, not accumulates. This is very different from what we are told under the current scientific and engineering paradigm. We are told that human knowledge is a pursuit, and that there is always more to know. We are told that we must continue to peel back the layers, and venture into new places to discover how nature works. We are told that knowledge is like an ever-expanding circle, whose boundaries reveal only more unknowns.

But if truth is invariant then further exploration only reveals what we already know. This is indeed much of what we see. Sure, newly discovered species in the depths of the ocean are things we have not seen before, and undoubtedly fascinating. But a new life form is a single instance of the same few processes that govern all life. There will never not be new life forms to uncover, but this does not mean we are learning anything fundamentally new.

Knowledge Growth versus Knowledge Convergence

Most of science and engineering has been about the accumulation and organization of knowledge. But knowledge only grows when it is of the reductionist kind. This is because reductionist knowledge is made of pieces and details, and there will always be more details to reveal. But if we are being intellectually honest about how nature works, those details do not map to the outputs we measure, observe and experience. The underlying assumption of reductionism is that pieces and connections reveal how the phenomenon of interest works. This is false.

The inner pieces we learn about are not responsible for the structures and behaviors of natural phenomena; not in the way reductionists believe. The story of pieces and connections leading to what we experience was only ever a convenient way to demarcate what we see and assign credit accordingly.

I have argued that emergence is the inevitable outgrowth of structures that process information to solve hard problems. Rather than some causal story from smaller pieces to bigger pieces, emergence merely finds the necessary configurations that map many inputs to fewer outputs. This kind of computing is all in service to the nested levels found within the structure of a natural problem.

Knowledge and truth outside reductionism are about invariance, and only that which persists is, by definition, invariant. This takes us away from the idea that knowledge grows. Rather than knowledge being about accumulating more information, it is about seeing the same patterns play out again and again.

This is a major shift in terms of what appreciating complexity brings to epistemology. Any theory of knowledge that rests on the causal connection between inner details and outer experience cannot be correct. The methods, validity and scope of what our current scientific and engineering paradigm brings to theories of knowledge are counter to how nature operates.

Framing knowledge in terms of a universe filled with yet-to-be-discovered truths is problematic. This is not to say there are no discoveries to be made, alas, the title of this book would make little sense. Rather it redefines what we mean by *discovery*. To discover is not to reveal some hidden inner details that make something tick, rather it is to *build* something that works. It is not about discovering new knowledge; it is about discovering solutions that operate to solve the challenges at hand. It is not mere praxis, which is the practical application of theory or knowledge, rather it is about building things. Our creative solutions cannot stem from preceding knowledge, it must emerge on its own accord.

Knowledge convergence is why philosophies that are thousands of years old still ring true today. The truths discovered during antiquity were invariant abstractions born from lives of turmoil. The inner details of those lives look almost nothing like modern man's, but the truths are just as relevant. This is not some attempt to connect philosophical truths to current technology, this is simply an undeniable aspect of how information operates in nature. Again, we cannot completely separate the informational from the physical, and the human attempt to do so is only one of epistemic convenience.

This does not mean we cannot be surprised about some new species in the depths of our ocean, or beneath the canopies of our rainforests. But when we look upon these species, the truest aspect of their physical and behavioral patterns are not so surprising. They are just another instance of nature's solutions, solving problems in its environment. These discoveries will always fall back to the same core truths.

Discovery in science and engineering is less about uncovering something we never knew, and more about exposing the same core patterns we see again and again. True knowledge, the kind most aligned with nature, converges rather than grows.

The Tyranny of Explanation

Science has made explanation its raison d'être. Its mission is to explain how the world works. We are told that the power of science lies in its ability to uncover the causal reasons behind what we observe. Science is here to reveal nature's secrets and use them to contribute to the growing body of human knowledge and our technological progress.

Resting the purpose of science on explanation is flawed. Explanation in today's science, while sounding like a worthy goal, fully depends on the notion of inner knowledge, making it primarily reductionist. To explain something scientifically, we are told, is to discuss how something functions internally.

An explanation puts forth a causal story about how outputs of a given phenomenon are produced. If we take a relatively simple system like an atom (simple relative to our experience) we can explain the colors we see in materials in terms of electronic transitions. Electrons are transitioning from different levels giving off photons of light at a given frequency, and our eyes perceive these frequencies as color.

But is this what color really is? Photon emissions undoubtedly play a role, but color exists in the realm of complexity, not simplicity. Perception, of anything, is far beyond some basic accounting of particles impinging upon our eyes. Our brains are processing and interpreting what we see.

Some will argue that we can always add more reductionism to our explanation, to try and account for what is missing. Beyond the physical properties of light, we can pick apart the biology of our visual system, and maybe add some psychology to explain the subjective interpretation of color. We can say that color perception involves a host of processes within the eye, including the absorption of light by photoreceptor cells, the signal processing by the retina, and the transmission of signals to what we call the visual cortex in the brain.

But what about factors such as lighting conditions, other surrounding colors, and individual differences in perception? We do not know if all people see colors the same way. There may even be some influence at a cultural level, lending to distinct associations and interpretations of what we see.

We can keep adding more explanations to account for the perception of color, but at what point does this become nonsense? While the emission of light frequencies by atoms is an aspect of color, it barely offers any explanatory power. Adding in the biological and psychological explanations only seems to muddy the waters.

The problem with reductionist explanations is that we can always make them. We can always choose a piece of the system and uncover its isolated existence. But this isolated piece is hardly an explanation for what we measure, observe or experience. In reality, the isolation of a thing tells us almost nothing about how things come to be. The only reason most people tend to believe in isolated causes is because we are assuming the isolated piece connects causally to perception. But it does not. It cannot. We know this, because in the complex regime pieces don't lead to the properties we perceive, not in any deterministic sense. And yet this is how explanations are marketed by the scientific enterprise. This assumed determinism is so baked into society's perception of science that when an explanation is provided, we presume it is causally connected to what we see.

The core fallacy with explanations is that, for complex phenomena, they cannot be tested for. Unlike a prediction, which can be tested by repeated observation, an explanation in the complex regime is highly immune to being destroyed. Imagine explaining the emotion of anger by measuring some activity in a region of the brain. Yes, the activity is real, as is its measurement. We can even refine the measurement to an arbitrary degree, adding increasing levels of precision to our explanation. But none of this can make the connection between the brain region and the experience more real. The actual connection between reductionist discoveries and human experience is largely fiction. It is based on an assumed causal connection that does not exist. We know it does not exist, because this is not how nature functions. Nature does not produce high-level things by using causal connections from lower-level things.

Consider Occam's razor, the problem-solving principle that recommends searching for simple explanations rather than more involved ones. The point of using simple explanations is not because they are easier to understand, or because simpler theories must be more true, it is because simple things can be *destroyed*. Occam's razor works because it admits epistemic humility, saying that we cannot know if something is true, but we can know if it survives. As I stated previously, things do not survive in nature for random reasons. Survival is the greatest testament to a thing's validity. But if explanations for complex phenomena are largely immune to being tested then Occam's razor goes out the window. Now explanations become propped up artificially, kept alive because of bogus assumptions about the discoveries being made; that they are causally and deterministically connected to what we experience.

None of this negates the epistemological necessity of ensuring we know how to distinguish justified belief from opinion. Yes, the inability to see causality inside complex systems means there is no way to test for a reductionist explanation. But there is more than sufficient reason to know such explanations are bogus. Not by testing with repeated observation but by resting arguments on *properties and logic*.

We know that complex phenomena have a host of properties they adhere to. These properties are emergent, and thus do not arise by some additive, deterministic set of inner steps. This is why there is no rational reason to accept electronic transitions as an explanation for color. Color has no meaning without perception, and perception is something that emerges from a complex phenomenon. No amount of additional physical, chemical, biological or psychological explanations can add to the picture of color, because there is nothing to add to.

To be clear, this does not mean electronic transitions, or any other biological, chemical or psychological mechanism is not playing a role. Of course they are. But *to know the role is to know almost nothing*. As argued previously, saying mitochondria produce energy is interesting, but has little meaning. This so-called "role" disappears entirely when the item is removed from the cell. Roles are convenient demarcations, not causal reality. If something fully depends on being embedded in a matrix of countless other roles, then the word role loses all meaning.

The tyranny of explanation is that it forces us to view the world through the lens of inner knowledge. It makes society accept only the disconnected mechanisms found through isolation and extraction as explanations for how the world works.

If the worst transgression of reductionist explanations were its fairy tale nature, they would be misleading at worst. But reductionist explanations work their way into our *designs*. Consider healthcare. Once a study has been conducted, showing some "statistically significant" result, it is often then folded into society. Researchers will isolate some aspect of a health-related phenomenon and confirm that it plays a role. This then becomes a *path* towards achieving human health. But just as inner knowledge of electronic transitions, while still being true in isolation, tells us virtually nothing about what color is, so too does the role of any vitamin, mineral or health-related intervention.

This is why explanations of complex phenomena must rest on properties and logic, not reductionist explanations. But logic alone cannot be the answer when it is used inside a broken paradigm. This is because logic only works when the premises that backup someone's statement are themselves valid. Someone can make a valid argument that they have uncovered the path vitamin C plays in health, but only because they are using premises that society incorrectly assumes are valid. This is how our reductionist paradigm gets away with so much nonsense. It is not the logic that is flawed. It is not that real discoveries are not being made. It is the baseline assumption that what has been discovered is automatically connected to the outputs we see.

But if logic is used *with* the properties known to be true in complex systems, then it becomes a powerful tool to make arguments about phenomena we observe. Logic, paired with a more proper form of knowledge, one that is based on invariant truths, is a powerful tool for reasoning about what is real.

Logic with Properties

Logic is reasoning conducted or assessed according to strict principles of validity. Logic provides a framework by which humans can backup statements rationally, lending to their acceptance as generally true statements. I say *generally*, because in the real world there is no such thing as pure deduction. There is always a fuzzy aspect to how true premises can be, which precludes the possibility of there being both purely true and realistic statements. Put another way, only extremely simple situations can be *proven* to be true, and reality does not consist of simple situations. This is why there is no such thing as scientific proof. Logical proof yes. Mathematical proof yes. Scientific proof no.

This means the strength of a real-world logical argument rests entirely on its premises. While the system of logic can stitch together our premises and conclusions, only the truth of premises can bind an argument to nature. It is the proximity of one's premises to what we know about nature that makes something more true.

Today's reductionist science will use logic (loosely and indirectly) to defend its position. Science runs experiments or develops theories, and these are done to support the truthiness of premises used in arguments. If someone measures activity in a region of the human brain, they will reason about how this activity can be used to infer a conclusion related to the source of some behavior. Perhaps fMRI scans reveal increased activity in the prefrontal cortex of participants during some decision-making process. Researchers will reason that the prefrontal cortex plays a crucial role in decision-making. So far, this is entirely valid. But this argument rests on a deeply flawed assumption about how nature works. It assumes (and in no way establishes) there is a neural *source* of human decision-making. In a fully baked argument, this would be another one of their premises. But this premise cannot be true. It cannot be true because we *know* that complex systems do not have sources. Complexity, by its very definition, rests on emergence, which does not function according to source locations or regions. Emergence is arrived at in a holistic, deeply interdependent fashion. The properties of complex systems, with the human brain being the most complex of all, cannot produce outputs using a region or a location.

The assumption that there must be a neural source of human decision-making is a hidden premise (also called an implicit premise). This is a premise that is not explicitly stated but is assumed to be true for the conclusion to be valid. Hidden premises are problematic because they go unnoticed and unexamined. This can potentially lead to faulty reasoning. In the case of so-called regions of activity that explain the outputs of a complex system, these hidden premises are downright false, making any conclusion drawn from such experiments bogus.

This is the rot at the heart of today's scientific and engineering paradigm. While reductionist premises worked perfectly fine in the discovering and building of simple things, they are false in the face of complexity. Today's science and engineering get away with so much reductionism because logic is not being used correctly to defend its conclusions. Most of the experiments and theories of today are running on arguments with hidden premises, rooted in reductionism.

To the laymen, such studies appear perfectly fine. Perhaps even ethical. If we are told that brain region studies reveal *how* certain individuals struggle with decision-making when this region is impaired, it suggests there might be a downstream treatment. But this is bad science finding its way into our designs. When it comes to intervention, this is a recipe for disaster, not ethics.

Again, this is not the fault of logic. This is the fault of grossly misunderstanding complexity. Logic is a powerful ally to human reasoning, but it is only as strong as its premises. The proximity of premises must be close to what is *known* about nature. And what we know are properties, not causes.

This comes down to what I call *properties over reasons*. There are not an unbounded number of properties to discover in complex systems, there are only a handful, and these few are all that are needed to make our most critical decisions in science, engineering and society writ large.

Properties are best defined in contrast to causal explanations. Producing a causal explanation involves identifying the underlying causes or mechanisms that produce the outputs we observe, in a given phenomenon or event. Causal explanations attempt to explain how something happens. We could explain how a metal expands when it is heated by discussing the increase in kinetic energy of atoms, which leads to more atomic separation.

In contrast, a *property* is a descriptive aspect of an object or phenomenon. It answers what an object is like, not how it produces its outputs. In our metal example, the fact that metal expands when heated is a property of metal (thermal expansion). Here, there is no appeal to causal mechanisms. Just the *fact* that metal expands when heated.

Properties can be thought of as constraints nature adheres to. Properties set the boundaries within which physical, chemical and biological processes occur. There are many properties in nature, such as how mass and energy cannot be created or destroyed, only transformed. How the total momentum of a closed system remains constant over time, unless acted upon by external forces. How entropy does not decrease in isolated systems, how gravity attracts objects with mass towards each other, and how electromagnetic forces bind small matter. Others relate to the process by which organisms pass on traits, and how those better suited to the environment tend to survive and reproduce. We know that ecosystems exhibit nutrient cycling and energy flow. We know there are constraints on the speed of light. We know that the properties of materials impose limits on what is physically possible. We know that systems in nature tend to seek equilibrium and stability through feedback mechanisms. And so on.

The previous properties are not *how* things happen, they are *why* things happen. In simple systems, the how and why are essentially the same. If I ask why planets remain close to the sun, the property of gravitational attraction can tell us both the how and why. But under complexity this is not the case. If we ask how *all* the planets remain in the positions they do, we can still answer the why (because of gravity) but we strain to answer the how (the specific process that keeps the planets where they are) in any exact sense. Extend this to more complex systems and the how disappears altogether.

We have seen the various properties of complexity throughout this book. These fall under the broader areas of thermodynamics, information theory, computation and evolution. I have discussed the evolutionary process, nature's recipe of variation, selection and iteration, the way entropy is tied equally to both the physical and informational aspects of phenomena, nature's use of information compression, the nested structure of problems, flexible determinism, multiple realizability, how meta-level processes create abstractions, group selection, and the fact that things do not survive for random reasons.

These all stem from more basic properties like nonlinearity, self-organization, adaptiveness, resilience, feedback loops, hierarchy, criticality, chaotic and periodic dynamics, synchronization, phase transitions, bifurcation and spontaneous pattern formation.

While this list might seem extensive, it is quite small in comparison to the number of causal explanations scientists and engineers put forward. There are no bounds on the number of explanations that can be concocted under reductionism. We can always peel back layers, choose to demarcate some bit of matter (genes, regions, etc.) and then invent a story about how it connects to what we observe at the surface.

I argue that truly rigorous scientific descriptions of things, and any decision making that might stem from them, cannot rest on causal explanations. It is far more properly scientific to describe and decide on nature based on its universal, timeless properties. Real world situations, and all of nature's phenomena, do not have paths and root causes, they have undeniable properties they adhere to. Properties are the invariant truths that exist in the abstract, which is where genuine truth lives. Only by a framework that pairs logic with properties, not reasons, can we enter an intellectually honest phase of science and engineering within the age of complexity.

The Direction of Complexity

What the properties of nature show us, which would be missed if we were mired in causes, is that there is a one-way direction to complexity. Complex things exhibit the sudden and irreversible emergence of physical structures and behaviors. The properties that we see in nature are not arrived at from some source or path, they materialize out from a fantastically intricate system of statistical likelihood. *All* the pieces are required to make nature what it is. Nature's solutions cannot, would not, function without the entire group working in concert to produce the holistic output. In simple systems, each piece adds incrementally to the functioning of the whole. That is not how complex systems work. Complex systems emerge in an instant, when the necessary pieces are in place to compute the answers to their external problems.

The utter absence of a deterministic path under complexity means complexity only operates in *one direction*. We cannot piece together the components that make a complex system work, rather complexity must arise after-the-fact. This precludes, completely, the notion that design can lead to good outcomes.

This one-way direction of complexity guarantees that a design will interfere with building complex things, by preventing emergence from happening correctly. This is why writing that uses upfront literary structures will produce boring content. This is why introducing a genetic change deliberately, to design some outcome, never works without side effects. This is why "precision medicine" is an oxymoron. This is why drastic social engineering will eventually lead to atrocities. Good design under complexity is not a matter of difficulty, but of impossibility.

Introducing changes to the inputs will, by definition, produce a wide range of changes to the outputs. A few of those changes may prove desirable. The headache might disappear, the corn fields may flourish, the baby might have blue eyes. This does not mean the cause has been identified, it just means turning a crank on one end of the system led to some reproducible change on the other end. DDT was highly effective in controlling mosquito populations, but also proficient at disrupting food chains, thinning eggshells and destroying populations. Everything is connected. Nature does not run on the fictitious causes defined by humans. Complexity does not run on a path from inputs to outputs in the deterministic sense. The intervention into complex systems is based on design, and design must interfere in a detrimental fashion, because it is based on a premise that is diametrically opposed to how complex systems produce their outputs.

Knowing the properties associated with complexity, and thus life, allows us to make better decisions based on universal patterns that are associated with complexity. All situations can be better decided on because, rather than resting decisions on fictitious inner knowledge (reasons), we base them on universally true properties that are guaranteed to hold. This does not guarantee specific outcomes, but it does guarantee that systems will adhere to constraints and patterns we already know.

Survival is the Only True Validation

Validation has always played a core role in design. Countless processes have been invented to help confirm that a design meets the needs and requirements of end users and other stakeholders. The point of validation is to ensure a design will solve the problem it was intended to address. Of course, all of this depends fully on the causal determinism of simple machines, which does not exist under complexity. Thus, what does validation mean when we build complex things? How can we know that our work is conforming to what is needed to solve the problem?

The key difference is that complex solutions cannot solve problems *as intended* (in the sense of a known process) because intention smacks of design. We cannot know any specifics regarding how the internal guts of our complex inventions solve problems because there are no "guts" in the reductionist sense.

And yet validation is important. We must validate the automatic realization of physical abstractions, which compute answers to naturally hard problems. We cannot write an entire book without some form of validation en-route to the end. We cannot engineer the next deep learning system without validating that our ongoing efforts are conforming to knowledge about systems. This is true, but what is critical is the *redefinition* of what constitutes *knowledge about systems*.

As discussed previously, it is the properties of complexity that now matter; that delineate good from bad solutions. These properties are what must be conformed to. But we must be careful with the word *conform*. Recall the direction of complexity. Validation under complexity can only work after-the-fact, not before.

Something conforms when it complies with rules, standards or laws. In the current science and engineering paradigm this occurs in the opposite direction to complexity. The rules, standards or laws used are set in place at the beginning, and our work is expected to conform to them en-route. In complexity such conformance must operate in the opposite direction. Rules, standards and laws must only be used as *signals* that our use of trial-and-error and heuristics is going well.

This is about making sure that the structures inside the guts of our creations *emerge*. The rules, standards and laws of conformity are only there to help signal that what we create is showcasing properties we expect. What makes properties, instead of reasons, work under complexity is that they do not interfere. Properties do not intervene on the organic flow and arrival of our creation's inner details.

This makes properties categorically *meta*. Take any property of complexity, say self-organization. This is self-referencing because it involves entities organizing themselves without external intervention. Self-organization leverages self-sustained feedback loops that enable the system to refer to itself for guidance and direction. How about multiple realizability, where different underlying structures produce the same outcome or behavior? Here, there is a kind of redundancy that allows a system to adapt by finding alternative "paths" to achieve the desired outcome. Again, there is no external intervention that tells the system where to go or how to change. It is the built-in capacity to map many inputs to few outputs that allows the system to self-adjust.

In contrast to design, building complex things is not about conformity, it is about taking more actions until the structures that emerge show signs that they are truly complex. It is not about expecting the structure of our creations to look a certain way, it is about seeing if they show the telltale signs of complexity, regardless of what emergent structure appears.

The ultimate validation of anything is survival. In writing, our work should be only what survives our intuitions and emotions. We are on the right track if things feel right. We consider it done when there is intuitive closure. Following intuition hardly sounds like a rigorous approach to building things, and yet such high-level, imprecise motivations are exactly why they are so powerful. Intuitions are not hand-wavy excuses for justifying decisions, they are powerful emotional cues that have evolved over millions of years. When we see intuition this way, we realize it is a potent guide to crafting complex objects. More to the point, this binds intuition to something mechanistic and rigorous; the properties of complexity. Intuition is implemented via heuristics and pattern recognition. Intuition is not some untethered ephemeral sentiment lacking rigor, it is an evolutionary trigger that operates far more effectively than anything offered by the so-called enlightened constructs of reductionism and precision.

Back to writing. The properties of complexity are all here, intuitively looked for when one writes well. Good writing leverages a great deal of nonlinearity, as the author bounces around the vast possibility space in an initially haphazard fashion. The words on the page eventually self-organize, as each iteration by the author acts as self-referencing feedback to improve content. The work begins to show resilience, as the author looks upon their work the next day with fresh perspective, retaining words that survive. Hierarchy forms naturally, as words materialize into paragraphs, paragraphs combine to form sections, sections aggregate into chapters. There are phase transitions in writing, where one's earliest ideas appear choppy and disjointed, with inconsistent pacing and awkward phrasing, only to get smoothed into a fluid phase over time. These are not forced analogies. The reductionist despises such emotive phrasing because it refuses to latch onto their isolated symbols and words of precision. But there is no ultimate distinction between the physical and informational. Intuition works because it taps into complexity. Period.

Regardless of the project, if what is being created is a truly complex object then it will show signs of complexity, and those signs speak to the fact that the topmost stressor of a hard problem, survival, is being resolved. This is true validation. Not designs, survival. We cannot know what a surviving, valid structure is supposed to look like. Our solutions must appear as nature's solutions; forever surprising in their appearance, yet unsurprising in the properties they adhere to.

Design tries to parrot the properties of complexity in a low-dimensional fashion and applies them in the wrong direction.

Design uses structure, organization, and even feedback, but it does so in an intervening and destructive way.

In the previous sections we saw how the properties of complexity allow us to make better, more logical decisions since our premises become far more legitimate than anything based on fictitious inner causal knowledge. Both science and engineering must align their work to making better arguments about why something is valid. There is no better argument than one based on what survives, and what survives is complexity.

How versus Why

In chapter 6 we saw the connection between the thermodynamic and information-theoretic versions of entropy. This connection allowed us to see nature for what it really is; entities that compute answers to problems. Thus, while we usually think of nature in terms of its physical processes, it is ultimately about processing information to solve problems.

The coming together of atoms into molecules solves the problem of fueling chemical reactions, adding structural support, bringing about function or enacting energy conversion. Yes, atoms adhere to each other through the interactions of electrons and nuclei, but that is how they come together, not *why* they come together. Atoms stick together for the purpose of forming an inevitable configuration of matter that processes information to solve a problem.

It is important to point out that when we isolate the physical realm into discrete pieces, we are losing the essence of *why* something is happening. In simple systems, such delimitation serves to bring forth a clean objectivity to how we understand the world, but when it comes to complexity such delimitation mitigates understanding. This is because the discrete interactions have almost nothing to do with why something came to be.

Changing our focus from *how to why* is one of the major shifts (both scientifically and philosophically) demanded by any intellectually honest account of reality. The formation of the structures we see in nature are the only ones that could have formed, not because of some unique set of interactions among its components, but because there can be no other configuration that solves the problem. Nature works in an automatic and inevitable fashion, not by reductionist reasoning, isolation and inner causality.

Atoms and molecules are one thing. What about the beaver, or some other highly complex thing; anything far beyond the scale of microscopic entities? It turns out that we can explain beavers with just as much rigor as atoms, as long as we are reasoning about the why, not the (conventional) how.

How, in today's scientific and engineering paradigm, asks about the specific manner by which something occurs. How does photosynthesis happen in plants? How does an engine create motion? How does one solve this mathematical problem? But the *why* relates to the rationale or underlying principles that lead to a given structure or behavior. The reductionist will spend their careers trying to answer *how* the beaver looks and acts the way it does. They will never bring a rigorous answer, because nature's solutions are not about causal chains, they are about manifesting structures that solve problems with flexible determinism. The beaver's set of configurations are the inevitable outgrowth of problem solving. Its set of features, and the way they're used, overlap, informationally, with the demands of its environment. That is it.

We can see the extreme universality of thinking of things in informational and computational terms. Under complexity, reaching inside the guts of a system is not going to tell you how that system works. The mechanism, and any rationale used to defend it, must be based fully on the logic of how informational and computational properties are satisfied.

Chapter 9

Life is Not a Game

Math as a Residual of Nature

Mathematics has been a part of science and technology for much of our history. Arithmetic was used by early civilizations for agricultural planning, trade and taxation. Geometry was used to plan and arrange materials for structures. Early calendars used mathematics to track the passage of time and understand celestial movements. Statistical methods and economic theories have been based on mathematical principles. Both Einstein's theory of relativity and quantum mechanics rest their foundations on mathematics. Early computers leveraged mathematical theories of computation.

Today, mathematics is often referred to as the purest of all sciences. The generally held perception is that mathematics is how we make science rigorous. The more precise and mathematical one can be about their theories, the more meticulous and careful they are with their reasoning. More to the point, mathematics is assumed to be the language of nature, since most natural systems showcase many of the symmetries and structures found in math itself.

But the truth is, when mathematics gets applied, its success is largely found in unnatural situations. Consider the game of poker. Mathematics can help a person win more games in poker by assisting their decision-making using probabilities and employing mathematical strategies. But poker is hardly a real-world situation. Poker has a set of easily followed rules; step outside those rules and you would not be playing the game correctly. Poker is a game, not life.

If this example seems too contrived, consider route optimization. Route optimization tries to find the best route among a large set of possibilities, something mathematics can help with. Route optimization is a categorically hard problem, and seemingly much more realistic than a poker game. After all, humans have always needed to find their way around. The possibility space in the find-the-best-route problem is massive, and there is no direct path to finding the solution. And yet route-finding is still a contrived thing. There are no routes in nature. The forest has foliage, canopies, shrubs and trees, leaves, branches, and various organic matter, but not routes. Routes are things made by humans, like trails, paths and roads. Routes are a byproduct of the low-dimensional workings of our modern world.

While both poker and route optimization have real world counterparts, such as negotiating the purchase of a car or finding the fastest way to work, they still operate inside relatively artificial situations. A car purchase occurs under the structured rules and social conventions involved in the buying process. This is not a situation with a ton of wiggle room, rather one where slight advantages appear and are exploited. Compare this to meeting a bear in the forest. There are no rules of engagement, only the instinctual recognition of patterns and emotional decisions to act quickly. But this does not mean there is no negotiation. One must consider the position, interests, and potential threats the bear poses. They must assess the threat level, behavior, and potential danger of the situation. We do not think of such things as negotiation, but only because they happen so quickly. We do not see the information used in any precise and mathematical fashion, but rest assured, it is being used.

The fastest way to work can be found through mathematical optimization, but only because we drive in a grid-like environment with well-defined rules. Mathematics gets applied to so many of our modern preoccupations because many of our circumstances have been set up like games. When something is a game, it has pieces that are visibly exposed and explainable. This simplicity is how math can *attach* itself to the parts of the system.

But as we move away from the realm of games, into more natural settings, we lose that attachability. What was distinct, transparent and controllable becomes smoothed out in the turbulence of complexity. Under complexity, math loses its grip on the systems it hopes to describe. This usually gets chalked up to mere approximation, but as I argued in chapter 5, complexity is not a supercharged version of deterministic systems, it is something different altogether. No amount of mathematics is going to help you negotiate a bear encounter, or find your way through a dense, untouched forest.

An obvious rebuttal at this point would be to defend applied mathematics under the premise that our lives are largely dedicated by modern game-like constructs. Most of us are not running into bears or scraping our way through forests to get to work. But the age of complexity challenges this framing. While it is true that our society has become increasingly based on game-like rules that lend themselves neatly to the mechanics of mathematics, things change drastically when complexity becomes our modus operandi.

Not only are we no longer looking to build simple machines, our reasoning about nature must now account for how complexity works. Complexity is not some niche area of science, it is everything. Our theories of nature, our definitions of knowledge and skill, and our application of softer, heuristic thinking is what now matters. This makes the use of mathematics to describe nature increasingly problematic as we begin to realize that complexity cannot be ignored.

But not all mathematics is ultra-precise and deterministic. Probability raises itself above precise predictions and deductions and instead tries to account for the uncertainty and randomness in the real world. With probability, we have a framework for quantifying and reasoning about unpredictable situations.

But probability still suffers from the attachment issue. In any probabilistic assessment there is the notion of something being divided by something else; as in two things being compared. If we wanted to calculate the probability of drawing an ace from a deck of cards, we would first identify the total number of possible outcomes (the denominator), then identify the number of favorable outcomes (the numerator), and finally divide the number of favorable outcomes by the number of possible outcomes. Thus, the probability of drawing an Ace (4 in a deck) from a standard deck of 52 cards is 4/52 (0.077). The only reason we can calculate our drawing-an-ace probability is because we can attach our probabilistic framework to the specifics of a game-like situation.

Sure, there are more advanced methods in probability than calculating basic ratios, but they all still make this kind of comparison. The use of probability means there is still an *implicit* contrast being considered between the likelihood of an event happening and the likelihood of it not happening.

A deck of cards is one thing, but now consider how unrealistic it is to make a comparison in a natural setting. The numerator would have to be the number of times some event happens, and the denominator the number of overall events that could take place. How could this comparison possibly be calculated? Perhaps a reasonable guess could be made for the numerator, but the denominator? No chance. There is no way to know the number of overall events that could take place, because the number of events is *virtually infinite* in natural settings.

If all this talk of ratios seems too simplistic to describe the essence of probability, we can move onto distributions. When we see a probability distribution plotted on a graph we are visualizing the values of a mathematical function, one that represents the likelihood of each possible outcome of a random variable (an unknown or changing quantity whose values are based on the outcomes of a random phenomenon). In other words, outputs produced by natural things.

Probability distributions are used by insurers to assess risks and calculate premiums, in financial modeling to manage risk, in quality control to monitor and improve product standards, in medical research, epidemiology, and clinical trials to analyze health-related data, to forecast weather conditions and supply chain demand, to optimize inventory, and in AI via its use of statistical methods and machine learning algorithms.

If probability is so limited in terms of its ability to reflect natural situations, then why is it used so predominantly? Because again, everything listed previously operates under the structured rules and social conventions of the world we have created.

Probability arose from gambling, which makes sense. Logically, the origins of something does not invalidate its use, but it does show us how probability was originally envisioned, as a tool for making decisions in games of chance. It is unlikely that probability ever would have been discovered inside a natural setting. This does not mean chance plays no role in the real world, only that nature's version of chance does not run according to the simplistic rules of a human-made framework.

Only games are confined enough to calculate a number that tells us the likelihood of something happening. This means that mathematics, including its probabilistic versions, are highly disconnected from what nature is, and how she works. If we operate in constrained environments, then mathematics is an excellent tool for making decisions and describing inner processes. But move into the realm of real-world complexity and mathematics loses its hold on how things function. This does not threaten the area of pure mathematics, which is only concerned with abstract concepts and theoretical consequences. But when it comes to mathematical application, including its use in fundamental physical theories, it suggests a profound limit to its validity.

When the things we build are simple, applied mathematics is highly relevant to our challenges, offering a rigorous way to reason about the design of our systems. But when we enter an age of creating genuinely complex things, the default assumption that mathematics is where we will find rigor is highly suspect.

Many understand the disconnect between mathematics and reality. Most students complain about the lack of utility of mathematics to their lives. This complaint is usually disregarded, using the usual excuse that mathematics, even if not directly applicable, gives us a better way to think. This might have been true during the Enlightenment and Industrial Revolution, but this statement does not hold up when what we build is genuinely complex. In fact, if we are being honest, mathematics can easily encourage us to think incorrectly, as demonstrated by the ratio example discussed previously.

It is not just students who notice mathematics' lack of real-world utility. If we look at those who use mathematics in the stock market, we see an advantage for those with the resources to squeeze out discrepancies between asset prices, or some other form of informational asymmetry. But these advantages are subtle, and only useful to those who have already considered things more fundamental. If mathematics were that formidable, many more would be making a killing in the stock market. The same holds for sports betting. There may be some slight advantage to those looking to make reproducible profits, but not enough to benefit most people. And all this still ignores the survivorship bias at play.

The underlying assumption that mathematics and probability map to the real world comes to us from an age when it did just that. But that is not the age we are entering. Barely squeezing out a profit from the market or a sports bet is one thing, but what about the creation of genuinely complex things?

The argument that our modern world makes game-like calculations useful is beginning to lose ground. STEM-related knowledge needs a major overhaul to stay relevant in the face of complexity. As we continue to raise the level of physical abstraction in the things we build we move further away from inner knowledge, towards things that become tractable by trial-and-error, heuristics and pattern recognition.

This is not so much an argument against mathematics, but rather how it is currently applied. Mathematics is more about abstraction than it is calculation, and abstraction is what complexity is all about. Not just informationally, but physically. But mathematics is largely wielded in the causal sense, as though it speaks to the inner workings of the systems we create; an approach that will prove utterly untenable in the age of complexity.

We are often told that AI is made possible by mathematics. After all, deep learning uses a variety of methods from linear algebra, such as matrix operations, vector spaces, eigenvalues and eigenvectors etc. Deep learning uses differential calculus with its gradients and derivatives, as well as integral calculus and optimization. There are distributions, expectations and variances from probability, Bayesian statistics, Markov chains, graph theory, combinatorics, and so on. One might be forgiven for chalking AI up to the implementation of mathematics in computing. It all seems like a great success story of applied mathematics.

In one sense this is true, but it is highly misleading. Mathematics is used to construct the scaffolding of AI systems, but it most definitely is not what makes AI work. AI works because of emergent properties that were not engineered into the system. Mathematics is akin to the individual ants of a colony. Individually, ants have important characteristics, but specific ants do not solve hard problems; the collection of ants do. It is the letting loose of countless "ants" that allow the meat of AI to materialize and compute the outputs needed. Mathematics is how we construct the individual pieces of the high-level process we need to enact: trial-and-error paired with heuristics. After that, the systems converge in ways we cannot understand in the deterministic, causal sense.

In order to put in place the scaffolding that ensures trial-and-error can happen inside software, AI engineers require a way to compute things like distances, rates and mixing. AI uses *distance* calculations whenever it attempts to close the gap between the model's best guess and the actual quantities or labels. AI uses *rates* when it leverages calculus to compute parameter values. AI uses *mixing* when it multiplies large matrices together to transform data. Math is most definitely being used in today's AI systems. But not because math is tapping into the essence of how complex systems produce their outputs, rather it is because math is our only way to code the distances, rates and mixing into the machine.

Math gives us a way to define distances, rates and mixing computationally. But the concepts of distances, rates and mixing do not belong to mathematics, rather they are necessary aspects of any process that looks to proceed via trial-and-error and high-level heuristics. There may be far better ways to enact distance, rates and mixing than anything mathematics can express or capture, but for now, math is all we have. The vectors and matrices of mathematics are useful, but there is no reason to believe their (potentially platonic) existence is how nature operates.

It is not math that makes AI tick, it is the concepts that lie at the heart of trial-and-error and the use of heuristics. Math must be understood as nothing more than a residual of what occurs in nature, not some definitive account of her inner workings.

But today's scientific and engineering paradigm is steeped in the assumption that math itself is how complex things function. We see this mentality in the ongoing discomfort today's scientists and engineers have about the "alchemy" of AI. It pains many in the scientific and engineering circle that AI appears more like an art than a science. AI systems are improved, not through careful design or deep causal reasoning, but by high-level mixing and matching, adding more data and processing power to achieve results. It all sounds so unrigorous.

It is the fight against the alchemy of AI research that is the problem. Today's AI researchers want to find a more rigorous description of how AI works internally. But there is nothing to find. We know how AI works, as long as we move away from the causal version of *how*. Only surface-level knowledge related to information, computation and evolution can describe what AI is doing. The academic exercise to reach into systems and find some deterministic story told by an elegant mathematical theory is bogus under complexity. Math is not how AI works, it is how AI is set up.

Mathematics being nothing but a residual of reality speaks to the nature of how we must build complex things. We have to reframe our understanding of what mathematics represents. It is not something that can describe how something complex works internally, nor can it guide us on how to build complex solutions. There will never be a *proper* mathematical theory about how the guts of complex things function. Mathematics, at best, is a useful tool for programming the kinds of computational scaffolds needed to ensure trial-and-error happens in a machine.

This dramatically changes the way we think about applied mathematics, and more broadly (and more importantly) what it means to bring rigor to science and engineering. Mathematics is not some universal language with which we can understand the universe, rather it is a framework for creating and thinking about computational constructs that set up systems, but do not govern their operation.

Nature Uses the Full Distribution

Despite mathematics and probability being inherently disconnected from how complexity works internally, probability does offer a useful analogical tool. We can think of nature's phenomena as producing her outputs according to a range of possible values. This is what probability distributions attempt to capture.

Most probability distributions have peaks, which are where the values are most concentrated. This means the peak/s is the set of values we are most likely to observe. We are most likely to observe those values because they occur with the highest frequency. If we roll a fair six-sided die again and again, we expect each number to appear roughly the same number of times, producing a uniform (flat line) distribution. But if we bias the die, making it land predominantly on the number 6, a peak will appear in the distribution of values, showing us that 6 is a more likely outcome.

We can connect the concept of peaked distributions to entropy and multiple realizability. The peak of a distribution represents the most statistically likely configuration. This is precisely how entropy maps an arrangement of pieces to a given macroscopic state. It is the arrangements that occur most often that lead to what we can expect to see. Inline with this is the concept of multiple realizability, which as you will recall, means that the most invariant properties in complex systems can be arrived at in the most possible ways. Since the peak of a distribution is what we expect to see and corresponds to the mechanism by which entropy lands on invariant structures and behaviors, it means we can think of the peak of a probability distribution as an emergent structure or behavior.

A critical realization in all this is that the peak is nothing without the rest of the distribution. The peak shows us what to expect, since it represents the most statistically likely microscopic configurations of the system. But this doesn't mean the other configurations aren't relevant. Quite the opposite; these less-probable configurations play a critical role in shaping the overall distribution. More to the point, the most probable configurations would not exist unless all the other configurations were present. Without these less likely configurations the statistical properties of the system would cease to exist.

Why is this relevant, and what does it have to do with building things in the age of complexity? It shows us that nature must be using the *entire distribution* to make complexity work. This has major consequences for the fallacy in modern science of trying to understand things through isolation. It shows us that reductionism, in all its manifestations, must be fundamentally wrong, because it is inherently disconnected from what we observe, measure and experience.

There is nothing "rigorous" or "scientific" about picking things apart in the attempt to reverse engineer nature. This is as true scientifically as it is for the things we build. I will elaborate on these consequences more later. For now, understand that the isolation done by reductionism does not even hold up to the mathematical and scientific principles the current paradigm supposedly adores.

Don't Run the Calculation

There are 2 ways we can use mathematics to make a decision. We can run the calculation and live by the results, or we can understand the universal properties that mathematics speak to. For the former, consider how mathematics and probability are applied today. In investing, we calculate expected return and risk across investments. In accounting we calculate results related to budgeting and financial planning. In engineering we simulate and analyze the behavior of structures under different conditions, analyze and manipulate signals, and study the stability and performance of various control systems. In science we simulate physical phenomena and predict experimental outcomes. In all these cases, the use of mathematics is to run calculations to get some result.

But the other side of mathematics is related to its properties, not its calculations. As discussed in chapter 8, a *property* is a descriptive aspect of an object or phenomenon. A property answers what an object is like, not how it produces its outputs. Mathematics is full of important properties that show us how a formal system behaves, and the constraints it adheres to. If treated as its own phenomenon, mathematics can elucidate important and universal properties of systems. Counterintuitively, this is more true for pure mathematics than it is for applied mathematics. Pure mathematics studies patterns inside math itself and does not attempt to reach into physical phenomena to describe what is happening, nor does it attempt to make specific tallies or predictions. Pure mathematics suffers less from its disconnect to reality, because it is not trying to discover anything other than its own internal outcomes. This arguably makes pure mathematics more relevant to building complex things than today's applied mathematics.

Despite being a mere residual of reality, mathematics need not be tossed aside. I have already shown how the conceptual understanding of probability distributions is a potent ally in framing how nature functions. But this is very different from running a calculation and seeing what spits out. Running a calculation to know the outcome of a complex situation suggests mathematics can tell us something it cannot. But appreciating the properties of mathematics can shed light on systems, because math is itself a system. A simple example is appreciating what probability says about the trade-off between risk and return, rather than attempting to calculate an actual risk value. The first one is a pattern that speaks to the dynamics of information, while the second one acts as though math itself reflects the internal workings of the system of interest.

Decision making under complexity should leverage the properties of math and probability, not their calculations. Calculations *enforce determinism onto systems*. It changes the decision-making framework from one that uses general behaviors to one that pretends to know what systems will do specifically. The former is a powerful tool for making decisions, the latter a dangerous and naive one.

Math is a residual of nature, but it is a system worthy of study, because it can tell us properties that are universally true. We can base decisions on math, by pairing its inherent properties, not its calculations, with the premises of our rational arguments. Beyond this, as I will discuss shortly, it turns out that mathematics can be more than just a description of patterns. It can in fact create things.

Gamification and Design

There is a direct relationship between the gamification of life and the notion of design. When we assume that the world can be modeled as games we port such models into the designs of our real-world systems. We assume that the visible causality inside games must also be there in complex situations, and that specific control over internals can still work effectively.

But the real world is not a messy extension of what we see in games. This is why taking what is found in the simplistic models of academia and applying them to real life is so deeply and profoundly problematic. As I discussed in my section titled Nature Does Not Approximate, nature is not doing what simple systems do, neither literally nor as an approximation.

To today's science and engineering paradigm the idea of not relying on inner causal knowledge sounds impractical. Where are the best practices? The design patterns? The industry standards? Are we supposed to just muck about and hope for the best? But the reality is this "mucking about" is far more rigorous than anything the current reductionist paradigm can offer. When we look at how genuinely hard problems are made tractable it becomes clear that naive action and pattern recognition is indeed the most efficient and effective way to build complex things. As discussed in chapter 7, what makes trial-and-error more tractable, even for humans, is operating at the highest level of meta, so as not to run into insurmountable computational limitations. By keeping problem statements as general as possible and creating highly flexible internals, mucking about becomes a far more effective means to build solutions.

Most engineers today would struggle to understand how AI could be done without design. Like all generations prior, they take their current starting point and attempt to design the next level of abstraction. Imagine an engineer working on improving a new memory structure, something like the matrix or tensor used today. They would call upon design principles and industry standards to structure their creation. In this case, the engineer is working on a single component of the overall system, and this piece itself is essentially deterministic.

But the role the memory structure plays can no longer be assumed. I will say it again: knowing something plays a role and knowing what that role is are two very different things. The so-called role of a memory structure loses meaning inside a complex object that *uses the full distribution*. The correct memory structure will be the one that emerges, when considered inside the context of the entire AI system. The only way for the correct memory structure to emerge is to *build it from the outside*, rather than being concerned with the specific design of a better isolated component. As argued in chapter 7, the internals of what we build must be flexible, not specific. It is not for us to know what the memory structure should look like, only that its emergence is part of a bigger picture.

Design is a byproduct of the gamification of life. It worked well for almost everything we have built throughout our history, because our world has been fashioned around the structured rules and conventions of simple machines. But complexity brings the behaviors found in real life closer to the way we build things. Design, like games, cannot make life tractable.

The Not So Surprising Reproducibility Crisis

There is a growing awareness of just how irreproducible much of science is. This obviously calls into question the reliability of the original findings published in scientific journals. After all, if we cannot reproduce what a scientist reports to have found, how can we trust that it was ever found in the first place?

The reproducibility crisis is known to be worse for the softer sciences. Psychology has been tainted with reproducibility issues since its inception. The fact that the softer sciences are more susceptible to irreproducibility is not surprising. Whereas a field like physics measures things against simple systems, fields like psychology attempt to measure and explain the mind, which stems from the most complex thing of all, the human brain. It is one thing for multiple scientists to measure the same frequency of light emitted from an atom but try getting many scientists to measure the same emotion, whatever that means.

Of course, this does not stop psychologists from trying to make their field something akin to physics, with its precise definitions and causal explanations. It is not enough to note the attributes of anxiety in individuals. To be considered a "real scientist" psychologists must make a causal connection between anxiety and some definition of distorted thinking. A set of root causes must be identified, and a story pieced together to show the path from source to outcome.

It is this physics envy in softer sciences that leads to their version of the reproducibility crisis, since one is attempting to measure things that are ill-defined. A behavioral scientist will attempt to show that human behavior has a root cause. They might measure some activity in a given region of the brain while someone is apparently exhibiting the behavior, in an effort to explain the neural mechanisms underlying the behavior. But the notion that human behavior has root causes is largely fiction, since this is not how complex objects produce their outputs. Add to this the challenge of knowing that someone is indeed exhibiting a specific behavior.

Regardless of the field, irreproducibility usually gets chalked up to poor scientific technique. Flawed experimental design, inconsistent or poorly defined methodologies, the misapplication of statistical methods, poor data management and reporting, differences in equipment calibration, and a host of cognitive biases are all deemed culprits of the reproducibility crisis.

But the true source of irreproducibility is the *lack of determinism* in nature. While reproducibility is deemed important for quality research, it is wholly unrealistic for anything but the simplest of systems. Reductionist science has chosen to define knowledge in terms of isolation and extraction. We are expected to control for variables, separate and confine regions of interest, and measure very specific things. But this is not how nature works. Nature does not have root causes and deterministic pathways. There is no reason to expect reproducibility in nature because, as per multiple realizability, there is no reason to think nature takes the same path twice.

Imagine 2 metal poles sticking out of the ground, about 4 feet apart. Now imagine I told you to stand a few feet back, and throw a frisbee between the poles, without the frisbee touching the poles. This is easy. But now imagine I move the poles closer together, say 2 feet apart. Now the challenge is more difficult, but still doable. But then I move the poles so that the distance between them is smaller than the diameter of the frisbee. We could still do it, by throwing the frisbee in a vertical fashion. But the more we constrain the system the more difficult it is to get the frisbee through the spacing.

Our poles and frisbee example is analogous to the mismatch between nature and the tools we use to measure nature. The poles are nature's phenomena, and our attempt to get the frisbee between the poles is our measurement. The more we artificially constrain phenomena via reductionism (move poles closer together) the less reproducible we can expect our measurement to be (getting frisbee through poles without touching them).

Reductionist science tells us to gamify the world, by isolating it, controlling it, constraining it. We place nature into labs and inspect its pieces, then expect others to measure the same thing. This is akin to moving poles closer and closer together and expecting many people to always throw the frisbee between the poles. Sure, an individual can develop "skill" in reproducing a good shot, but getting many people to do this is unlikely.

Humans are not meant to be working inside confined settings. Humans, as one of nature's solutions, are highly flexible. We operate best in complex environments solving categorically hard problems. We have many ways to throw a frisbee, including backhand, forehand, flick, hammer, thumber, upper hand, roller, overhand, push, etc. This is because humans are high-dimensional, and we are meant to operate in settings that are as high or higher in dimension than we are; to fill the space of possibilities with our abilities. But as soon as a *game* is created, we are confined to operate within constrained rules. The more gamified the environment the more we must artificially restrict our natural abilities.

Reductionism gamifies nature. It squeezes it into confined spaces and pretends it is far simpler than it is. By doing so we can get away with precise measurements, because we are now acting as though nature is itself precise. But nature is not precise. Sure, physics can measure things like the gravitational constant, the speed of light and the fine-structure constant to several decimal places, but these are disconnected from *how* nature functions. They do not have meaning by themselves. They are but pieces that get statistically smeared into the ill-defined aggregations of nature. They are not causal in any meaningful way. Physics is more reproducible only because it more artificially defines nature. Any other science that follows suit will run into reproducibility issues as the complexity of its phenomena increases.

Attempting to do better science, by today's definitions of better, will not help an honest study of nature. No amount of improvement in experimental design, consistency in methodology, appropriate use of statistics, better data management, superior equipment calibration or reduction in human bias can fix the problem. It is the reductionism that is at fault, because it creates a mismatch between what we are studying and our ability to measure it.

Science is a story of creating measuring tools that are constrained, in order to make precise measurements. But this constraining of our tools is no different than forcing our frisbee throw into a lower-dimensional, unnatural form. The hidden and faulty premise that isolated pieces speak to aggregate structure and behavior (i.e. the real world) is what has allowed science to get away with their precise measurements. Physics can get away with it because they are mostly interested in non-complex things to begin with. But the same cannot be said as we move up the ladder of complexity. Chemistry should be expected to be less reproducible, biology even less so, and the social sciences extremely so.

As long as researchers all act like physicists they will be constraining nature far too much to be measuring much of consequence, let alone things reproducible. A behavioral scientist using an fMRI machine to isolate some region of the brain is changing their frisbee throw to a very specific type to get it through the poles. The measurement can be made, but it operates inside a gamified version of nature.

This point is missed by most scientists. We know this, because the problem is almost always attributed to error in technique. But the problem is not the techniques used, it is the gamified foundation that today's science rests on. The absurdity gets demonstrated with the use of AI in science. Applying AI as a tool in science makes sense. AI can detect patterns that humans miss and find correlations among massive datasets. But those who apply AI to their scientific research are running into the same old reproducibility problems, with researchers failing to reproduce a good number of studies. This gets attributed to things like AI hype leading to overly optimistic expectations, lack of documentation on how models are created, and various sources of "leakage" such as when data used for training the model overlaps with data used for testing it.

But AI as a tool cannot be constrained the way other tools in science can. This is because AI is itself a complex object, something much closer to what nature is. Trying to force AI down to the low dimensionality of reductionist science is to force the frisbee player to only throw in a very specific manner. AI researchers having reproducibility issues is wholly unsurprising. Not because of overly enthusiastic feelings, lack of documentation or data leakage, but because AI cannot operate effectively in constrained environments. It was never meant to. Recall the deep learning solution for the Rubik's cube; AI will be as flexible as it can be, as long as the system it models is itself complex. The reproducibility crisis is just another byproduct of gamifying our world.

Does science need reproducibility? It would seem obvious that scientists should reproduce the work of others to confirm findings. But what findings are we talking about? Isolated structures and causal explanations are not what we need. We need things that work. Things we build. And the things we build are not to be replicated, they are to be realized in many different ways. The knowledge we need is not confined pieces of reproducibility; it is meta-level properties that are shown to hold true (survive) across many different instances. Inline with redefining knowledge is the necessity of reframing what it means to discover.

Starting Points of Computation

Mathematics is a residual of nature in the sense that it expresses some remnant of a deeper truth. Math's connection to nature is supported by the correspondence we see between mathematical and natural patterns, and the fact that mathematical models can find solutions inside complex spaces. The residual aspect is demonstrated by the degradation of mathematical explanation and prediction outside simple, gamified systems.

This is why I believe mathematics is best thought of as one of many phenomena worth studying, rather than some universal language that underpins nature itself. Mathematics lands on repeatable and recognizable patterns as one rearranges its symbols into new forms. This means mathematics can be expected to have its own meta structures and can bring forth discoveries via its self-consistency and built-in invariant patterns.

This seems to suggest that math is discovered rather than invented. This is a long-standing philosophical debate that contrasts two possibilities: 1) that mathematical truths exist independently of human thought, and we merely discover these truths through exploration or 2) mathematics is an invention of the human mind, developed as a convenience to describe and understand our world.

I propose that the discovery versus invented question is in fact the wrong one to ask. It is a philosophical paradox, which seems to suggest both answers cannot be true. But paradoxes only come about from inside the systems that express them, not when we step outside systems to comment on their validity.

Consider that mathematics may be nothing more than a reflection of how the mind arranges thoughts and finds logical consistency. To use mathematics is to hold a mirror up to our own thinking, where the rules and structures that keep mathematics self-contained are the very constraints that make human thought possible. If true, it is likely that mathematics emerged as a byproduct of the self-referencing complex objects regularly undergo.

As stated in chapter 7, going meta is how the physical abstractions of complexity are created. Complex systems fold-back-in on themselves to establish their emergent structures and behaviors. The human brain "observes" itself in the meta sense, as do all complex objects, but with a sentient mind this self-referencing produces human-level awareness. Beyond the raw mechanistic version of self-referencing seen in all nature's solutions, humans externalize theirs as symbols drawn on paper. To use mathematics is to take the same constraints the mind uses to harbor emergent reasoning, and wield it ourselves.

This does not make mathematics less interesting or less important. After all, human thinking is all we have, to reason about how and why our world works. But it does keep mathematics relegated to the phenomenon of human thought, rather than some universal language that underpins all reality. This is not as limiting as one might think. For mathematics unleashed within computing brings about a great deal of flexibility, as demonstrated by today's AI systems. As already discussed, what makes AI tick is not mathematics itself. Computing constructs are created using mathematics, but the system is let loose and allowed to converge on its own. Mathematics merely serves as the rules that enable data to be mashed together, but this mashing leads to the emergence of things not found in the mathematical language.

This makes mathematics more of a creative thing than a descriptive thing. Mathematics is how we set up machines to undergo mixing and matching. The properties of mathematics help us determine how such mixing and matching might happen. What this is not, is the internal rules of mathematics lending its symbolic reasoning to the systems we build. This is why symbolic AI never worked to solve hard problems, but today's connectionist AI does.

The fact that mathematics is a mental reflection of the constraints used by the human mind, and that those constraints are what bring about the flexibility seen in complex systems, brings us to *why* mathematics is a residual of nature: mathematics represents the starting points that nature uses to achieve emergence, but it does not represent emergence itself.

Since mathematics can only represent the starting points of complexity, and not provide the actual mechanisms by which nature works, this means that the natural home of mathematics is in computation. Recall from chapter 3 that the processing that occurs in nature means nature is computing. But nature computes using its emergent physical abstractions, not some deterministic machine that bumps pieces into pieces. Mathematics belongs to computing because its residual form represents the starting points of emergent computation.

We see paradoxes arise in mathematics because it is being incorrectly applied within the language itself, instead of being unleashed as creative fuel for emergence. The discovered versus invented debate is only a paradox when viewed in a non-meta fashion. This is in fact true for all paradoxes. Paradoxes are resolved when viewed outside the language, because the supposedly mutually incompatible sides are mere facets of the larger truth; one that can only be seen from the outside.

Mathematics says something is true if it does not lead to a contradiction. This is why methods like *Reductio ad absurdum* (Latin for "reduction to absurdity") are used to establish a claim by showing that the opposite scenario leads to contradiction. Inside a formal language, things are expected to work consistently and completely. Gödel's incompleteness theorems notwithstanding, mathematics operates under the premise that things can be proven true via their lack of contradiction. But it is the constraints of mathematics that make deeper truths appear as though they are contradictions. The inherent simplicity of mathematical reasoning, relative to how nature functions, leads to clashes between formalized entities. But step outside the language and contradictions disappear.

If we say "this statement is false" we will call it a contradiction or paradox. All paradoxes are of this essential nature, whereby pieces of the system appear mutually incompatible. But the fact that we can look upon such a statement and still reason about it means operating externally, outside the system we are commenting on, alleviates the paradox. For example, the statement might speak to something higher-level, something that is meta to the statement itself. Imagine our real purpose was to highlight the topic of contradiction, as we are doing now. Now the statement is perfectly logical, because it serves as a demonstration of a higher-level realization. A more philosophical example might be the seemingly contradictory belief that there is a God but also suffering in the world. Inside the system, God and suffering indeed present a paradox, but outside the system it can be rationally argued that suffering might serve a greater purpose (e.g. finding meaning in life).

Mathematics is not adversely affected by its inherent incompleteness because its true utility does not come from its internal rules, rather it stems from something else; that *something else* being computation. The contradictions inside math cannot interfere with computational reality because such a reality exists outside the mathematical starting points that breed its existence. This is true of any system under complexity. In real life, creative flexibility is made possible by a system's constraints, not through unbounded freedom and autonomy.

If the proper home of mathematics is computation, then why is most of mathematics and its use in theories not about computation? Einstein's Relativity does not speak of computing, it uses mathematics to describe space, time and gravity. How and why would Relativity be a residual of computing?

If mathematics is nothing more than a reflection of how the mind arranges thoughts, then it stands to reason that the symbols we use in mathematics are part of the brain's computation. If those parts of computation are mere starting points, as I argue, then Einstein's mathematics can be considered as starting points to *computed* Relativity. In other words, if let loose through computation we can expect Einstein's equations to manifest realistic aspects of space and time in software. This is not so controversial a statement. Nature can be thought of as computing, and thus Relativity, like any other phenomenon, can be thought of as a computation. We can simulate Relativity in computers by processing the underlying equations of Relativity in software. What is critical to realize here is that we are not running some calculation to determine anything specific, we are manifesting relativistic realities inside computers, via computation. One wonders if there is in fact much difference between what is created through computation and what exists in our physical worlds.

Up to now we have seen the need for a critical shift in science and engineering, and how we go about building things for the age of complexity. I have explored the essence of a hard problem, demystified emergence via physical abstraction and information compression, and argued for a more rational and natural approach to building things and making decisions. I have argued that the usual demonstrations of rigor in science and engineering, like mathematics and precision, are in fact mere residuals of a deeper reality. We are now ready to see how this foundation sheds light on some of our most critical social, economic, political and technological challenges.

PART 4
CONSEQUENCES

Chapter 10

Flawed Gatekeeping

A World Running on Design

Design tells us that we can reach into the guts of systems and reason about their inner causes. Knowledge defined in this fashion leads to a society built largely around reductionist science and traditional engineering. We are told that academia provides us foundational knowledge and skills to create solutions in the real world. We are told that to be "smart" is to have detailed knowledge about the inner workings of phenomena and systems. We are told that there are root causes to everyday situations, and that our ability to understand and control pieces means we can control the whole.

According to today's economy, a person understands their field if they know the inner details of the systems they interact with. A doctor learns the inner workings of the human body. An MRI technician learns the inner workings of the MRI machine. A mechanic learns the inner workings of the automobile. An economist learns the inner workings of the economy. In every profession, knowledge and skill is based on a foundation of inner knowledge.

But what happens when the whole premise of internal knowledge goes away? When the systems we create are no longer dependent on their inner workings? When the story about how things work cannot possibly rest on the guts of the systems we use? What does that mean for our ideas about knowledge and skill? What does that mean for the way we filter society based on merit?

In reality, a medical doctor's detailed knowledge of the human body does little to make them a good doctor. Effective doctors intuit the connection between symptoms and lifestyle, using high-level patterns to prescribe correctly. Good doctors relate to their patients and feel their way through challenges. An MRI technician does not need to know how their machine works in any detailed sense, only how to operate it effectively and produce good scans. As per progress by abstraction, real skills apply to high-level interfaces, not internals.

In the age of complexity, hard skills (as currently defined) become meaningless, because they are defined in a reductionist and causal fashion. Knowing the inner workings of the tools we use cannot enable us to wield them better, nor allow us to create the next level of abstraction.

And yet today's gatekeepers to opportunity are all centered around the notion of hard skills. Those looking to enter the workforce and contribute to the economy must work their way through an education system that rewards inner causal knowledge. This is not just for STEM fields. Social sciences, art, theater, etc. all operate under the premise that their areas of study can be picked apart and inspected. That there are causal reasons for producing good work, and that to be educated or professional means using this knowledge to make progress.

Our world is set up to reward and promote the wrong kind of skills. This works its way into industry, into the products we build and the services we deliver. In the age of complexity, it produces a glut of sterile talent and outdated expertise. It is not enough to make people aware of the differences between simple and complex systems. The paradigm needs an overhaul, where the skills we have evolved for are given back their rightful prominent place. Where our notions of merit rest on society's ability to form effective groups and build complex things. Where we eschew notions of root cause and designed outcomes, and instead fashion logical arguments using known properties of complexity.

Nerdism

Today's society celebrates the nerd. A nerd is someone who is usually good in a STEM-related field (or perhaps magic card games). The prototypical nerd is antisocial, likes details and appears interested in puzzles, more than getting along with others. Society has been conditioned to appreciate nerd-like behavior because nerds, we are told, are those who use their smartness to build our best inventions and usher in progress.

For most of our history this was true. Since the next level of abstraction was always designed, detail-oriented individuals excelled. But today, such behavior runs counter to building complex things. Detailed knowledge is precisely what does not lead to the kind of creativity needed. We are no longer in the business of building simplistic bridges and rocket engines, we are in the business of engineering emergence. What we need are people who can create the way nature creates.

This is not some mere annoyance with social awkwardness. Nerdism is a damaging ideal, because it places the wrong people into positions of power. CEOs of tech companies often have a nerd-like demeanor, because they are deemed safe, and rose the ranks via their engineering prowess. This kind of behavior is based on isolated facts and figures, not holistic truths and high-level properties. In the age of complexity, nerd-like behavior is a detriment not an asset. Today, we need those who can rise above the details and solve things in aggregate.

Nerdism brings the wrong kind of behavior into the upper echelons of society. This is dangerous to a world that now must tackle genuinely hard problems, by building truly complex things. Nerdism can only lead to fragile systems in the face of truly hard problems.

A common association made is the connection between nerds and high IQ. We are told that high IQ individuals are those with above-average ability to reason, learn and solve problems. In short, high IQ people are "smart." In reality, high IQ individuals are those who score significantly above average on standardized intelligence tests. This is a very different thing than someone being smart. Standardized tests measure against the bell curve and use an average to place people above or below some threshold of performance.

The problem here is that intelligence most definitely does not operate in accordance with a bell curve. Bell curves arise from additive processes, like taking all the heights of people in a room. The human brain is everything the bell curve is not. The human brain is the very essence of complexity, with an astounding number of pieces and connections, and our leading example of a complex object operating by emergence. What emerges in the human brain is most definitely not some simplistic, and highly convenient, average. In addition, recall from chapter 9 that nature uses the full distribution. This means that even under the assumption that human performance fits an average, it is the entire population that solves problems, not individuals.

High IQ can in fact be seen as a kind of mental deficit. Just as the left of the bell curve's peak can be considered mentally below average (as the IQ test was originally designed for), those who rank to the right of the peak can also be considered mentally challenged, in a different fashion. We did not evolve to think slowly and analytically about problems because natural problems cannot be solved by such approaches. High IQ individuals are very good at solving narrowly defined, gamified versions of life.

But rather than assigning individuals to buckets of ineffectiveness, it is more rational and scientifically correct to realize that all individuals in a population are required to solve hard problems. If the bell curve (or whatever distribution we use to model reality) appears, it is because nature kept it (all of it) around for a reason. That reason is survival.

Nature selects at the group level. Any truly rigorous account of human intelligence would never suggest that one sliver of the distribution among a group of people are the smart ones. Nature uses the entire distribution of human learning to solve problems. This is an undeniable fact based on known properties of information, computation and evolution. This is how nature solves problems. The notion that we should filter society based on some isolated piece of a distribution is reductionist hubris at its finest.

To be clear, we can still be nerds. But *nerdism* is the notion that only nerd-like individuals are smart. In the age of complexity, nerdism causes society to filter groups in an unscientific and highly damaging fashion. Nerdism means taking a thin slice through nature's full problem-solving distribution and artificially selecting talent. Nerdism is akin to creating flat faced bulldogs who cannot breathe. Artificial selection focuses on specific traits that are deemed desirable, at the expense of the overall health of the system. It is time for nerdism to be replaced with a deep appreciation for how nature *always* uses the group.

Cherry Picking the Parts that "Work"

A consequence of choosing design over discovery is the cherry picking of parts we want to keep. This violates the group selection that nature uses to solve problems. The academic narrative chooses the best parts of a topic and presents those to students, leaving out almost all the context that drives those key insights. No different than utopian ideologies that isolate the pleasant parts of society, without realizing the nice parts are made possible by the messy parts.

Consider the observation that lifting heavy objects leads to muscle growth. This realization can induce exercise in an individual, undoubtedly a healthy habit. But this can become a lesson in over-optimization. One often starts by targeting muscle groups individually; a "leg day" and an "arms day." Eventually the body becomes a collection of individually enhanced muscles. But a weightlifter's body can be less capable, and even fragile, compared to a more naturally fit physique (e.g. a farm boy). While the weightlifter's body has become very well suited to the weightroom, it is less so elsewhere. There is a reason our ancestors did not look like bodybuilders; such a physique would not handle most natural environments.

Again, group selection. Nature uses the entire distribution to solve problems. A healthy body is one whose muscles are strong but distributed. They are not all prominent, and they most certainly do not take on the extreme separation we see in those who over-optimize their bodies.

Recall that entropy leads to nature realizing the most probable configurations we see in systems, and that these most probable configurations cannot exist properly without the other parts of the distribution. A weightlifter optimizing muscle groups in isolation is akin to thinking only the peak of a distribution is needed (or perhaps something to the right of the peak). In terms of muscularity, there are many other hidden contributions that make a strong body truly strong.

It is well known that bodybuilders look stronger (by modern standards) than they are. Get a farm boy to challenge a bodybuilder to a strength contest, and the farm boy usually wins. What works to solve natural problems is the full distribution, not isolated and enhanced pieces that look separated. Complexity is comprehensive, broad and all-encompassing.

Chapter 11

Vicious Cycles

Circularity and the Undead

The only true validation to something's worth is its survival. A thing cannot remain in a natural environment unless it has something that works; unless its structures and behaviors reflect the problems that are presented by its environment.

Much of science and engineering has become circular. This means that progress is often framed in terms of what *helps the field* rather than what solves a real-world problem. Consider that almost no progress has been made in genetics in terms of curing or even reliably treating diseases. And yet we hear of advances in genetics all the time. But this version of progress is of a circular kind, where advances represent things that make the current paradigm more efficient. Consider advances in genetic separation techniques or imaging technologies. This sounds promising to most, since these advancements contribute to a deeper understanding of genetic materials and cellular processes. But that last statement is a reductionist one. Peering into isolated structures more deeply, and calling this progress, hides the premise that reverse engineering nature can tell us about the underlying mechanisms of things like disease.

But a better ability to isolate and view things on a small scale does not map to the outcomes we experience in real life, for all the reasons discussed in this book. We need not pick on genetics. The overwhelming amount of science that occurs today is based on the same bogus premise. The focus on reductionist progress keeps a good deal of science around that should not be. Institutions get away with calling many things "advancements", when in fact they do little more than reinforce bad narratives about how progress and complexity happen.

This brings us back to *going meta* as the ultimate approach to validate anything we build. We cannot validate something inside the system, only outside. This is the only way to protect the pursuit of knowledge from outdated paradigms that have run their course. One must look from the outside-in to realize whether an approach is worthy of continuation. Using the current paradigm to validate what we do never gets us out of the trap of circularity.

Let us return to the so-called intelligence quotient (IQ), and the research efforts focused on its use. If you debate a proponent of IQ, arguing that it does not hold up to any scientific notion of intelligence, they will point to statistical studies that show various correlations. These correlations try to associate IQ to things like academic achievement and occupational success. These correlations are what IQ proponents use as premises in their arguments. From this stance, only if one can show that the statistical methods are somehow flawed (e.g. correlations not statistically significant) will an IQ proponent concede that perhaps IQ is itself a flawed notion.

But this kind of validation is *not even wrong* because the paradigm itself is what is flawed, not the statistical approach. Just as someone who believes in a conspiracy theory can always make a logically valid argument, so too can anyone in the sciences, *as long as they stay inside the system.* In the case of IQ studies, the correlations appear by design, since what a high IQ really says is that *someone who is good at taking tests, is good at taking tests.* If society uses test-taking to filter access to opportunity, then rest assured IQ will correlate to academic achievement and occupational success.

This is why validation *must* occur outside the system, as this is the only way to avoid circularity. If we step outside the system on the IQ debate, we realize that the problem is not the statistics, which work perfectly fine in a self-consistent fashion, but rather the *application* of those statistics to the complex regime. This parallels the discussion in chapter 9 on how circularity within formal systems (e.g. paradoxes) can only be resolved by going meta.

It is circularity, achieved by never stepping outside the system, that allows many things to appear as though they are surviving, when in fact they are not. They are as the undead; kept alive by false hidden premises in an otherwise valid argument.

Magic as The Scientist's Strawman

Complexity is not the answer today's scientists and engineers want. Complexity is opaque and filled with uncertainty. Complexity does not appease the reductionist's need for inner knowledge and control, because complexity is the antithesis of such simplicity. Scientists have been told that knowledge about our world comes from peeling back layers and digging deeper; that to uncover how things work we must reveal the pieces inside.

This is why any explanation resting on complexity often gets dismissed by today's scientists as a kind of non-answer. Today's paradigm works under the premise that to know nature is to draw a causal picture from her inputs to outputs. All sciences, from the hardest to softest, want precisely defined things and neat causal stories. They all have a degree of physics envy. Anything else is deemed unrigorous and unscientific.

Operating under such a premise makes one chalk up complexity to little more than an appeal to magic. After all, if something cannot be explained causally then what is the explanation worth? But recall from chapter 8 that the problem with reductionist explanations is that we can always make them. We can always fold isolated pieces of a system into an explanation, because the current paradigm assumes pieces connect to the aggregate. The role of some reductionist discovery can be real, and yet still disconnected from things consequential to what we experience.

This makes the current paradigm's unwillingness to accept complexity a kind of *straw man* argument, that avoids accepting the lack of visible inner causality in virtually all of nature's phenomena. Rather than refuting the actual arguments based on known properties of complexity, many scientists today attempt to refute something else; something overly abstract or magical.

But the fundamental disconnect between pieces and observable properties destroys the antiquated notions of science and truth that reductionism rests on. A lack of causal story is in fact more scientific than some fairy tale about pieces bumping into each other to produce what we see. Nature works by manifesting configurations of matter that compute answers in multiply realizable ways, not through simplistic paths and root causes.

Chalking up complexity to a non-answer is a fully distorted version of the more intellectually honest and rigorous arguments made using the properties of complexity. This means criticizing today's science requires no transcendent authority. Nothing grander than the pursuit of science itself. The reliance on reductionism and consequent dismissal of complexity only serves as a cover for blatant failings. Much of today's science is kept alive through prestige, awards and outdated notions of rigor, rather than an honest account of how nature works.

Science itself, when validated as a process, already shows us the fatal flaw introduced by the so-called Enlightenment. Extraction, isolation and refinement take us away from what is observed, not towards it. Society assumes a natural flow from discovered pieces to human experience, yet no such connection exists. This leads to the layman believing something wholly unscientific, promulgated by a self-serving scientific enterprise that has made far less progress than its annals would suggest.

It is not magic that makes the complex world unexplainable, it is the distinct properties that emerge at the scale of everything that has physical consequence. No amount of digging can uncover a causality that is not there. There is no path from pieces to properties. There are no atoms of behavior. No line has ever been established between the guts of physical systems and the surfaces and essences of everything that is.

Science itself already marks the current paradigm as dead. Not magic. Science. There is nothing intellectual about dismissing the critiques against science as meaningless abstraction. That is a crutch, a distortion, a pathetic misrepresentation of science itself. Those who load up on contrived categories and precise symbols to "explain" our complex world are the real ones reading the tea leaves. Divining the interpretation of our world through the detached mechanics of reductionist analysis is the real mysticism.

The (Mis)Education System

The difficulty in achieving escape velocity from our current reductionist paradigm is largely due to our education system. The entire premise of education, what I call the academic narrative, is based on the idea that a strong connection exists between an educational foundation and real-world innovation. This is no different than suggesting one needs a plan to build things. Only if the isolated topics contained inside textbooks can be placed into designs does a foundation of education make sense.

Enter the age of complexity and the academic narrative loses steam. There is an increasingly severe disconnect between what is taught in school and the type of knowledge and skill needed to solve today's challenges. This is not merely a problem of unrealism; it is the fact that the academic narrative is diametrically opposed to the direction of complexity. From chapter 8 I argued that complexity operates in one direction. The structures and behaviors that enable complex things to solve problems arise after-the-fact. Just as this fully precludes the notion of design under complexity, so too does it invalidate the academic narrative.

Decisions about how to go about building things can no longer be based on the disconnected inner knowledge taught behind ivory towers. The task at hand is not about placing existing knowledge into higher-level constructs, it is about having higher-level constructs emerge on their own. To build as nature builds, the next generation needs to embrace naive trial-and-error more than the isolated facts contained in textbooks.

The best education one can possibly achieve is through the building of real things. When we create, we learn in a far superior fashion to anything textbooks and teachers could impart. This is because to build something that works is to make deep intuitive connections to nature. By working as nature works, through trial-and-error and heuristic reasoning, we understand the universal properties that nature adheres to. It is not a skill of memorized facts and figures, it is one of deep intuition and real-world application. This will be what it means to be truly rigorous and proficient in the age of complexity. Just as the best doctors and technicians showcase the softer side of problem solving, so too must subsequent generations of professionals.

Despite the education system running counter to how real life plays out, we are told the opposite. We are educated to believe that knowledge about smaller pieces maps to knowledge about how bigger things work. During the industrial revolution this was of course true. The machines we crafted had few components relative to what we build today, and those components bumped into each other in a deterministic fashion. To learn about the pieces that went into the systems we built was a worthwhile version of knowledge. But as we pass the threshold towards solving truly hard problems, requiring us to build truly complex things, academia as it currently stands is invalid.

In chapter 10 I argued that the filtering conducted socially by today's institutions is deeply problematic. Those with high grades are given the biggest opportunities to excel in life. The gatekeepers to opportunity are centered around the idea that passing exams signals intelligence and thus overall potential. But exams can only ever be an extremely narrow definition of smartness and promise. Given the group selection and multiple realizability of nature's solutions, we should expect the variety of skills and experiences that exist within a student population to be equally effective. It is the group that solves the problem, not the individual. Today's academia poisons the potential of society to solve problems because it takes a reductionist and unscientific approach to defining human potential.

The reality is that people can achieve the same outcomes in entirely different ways. This is not a motivational quip, this is mechanistically how nature functions; period. Today's education system is a consequence of outdated science and a broken paradigm. While its underlying premise made sense when we built simple things, it now runs directly against how society must build things going forward.

PART 5
PHILOSOPHICAL IMPLICATIONS

Chapter 12

Beyond Blueprints

Complexity is Simpler than Simplicity

Complexity gets talked about as though it is something that is difficult to deal with. This thinking stems from the false idea that complexity is a more difficult version of what we see in simple systems. Only the attempt to wrestle with an immense level of details does an activity become difficult. But chasing details in complex systems and situations is akin to chasing ghosts. It makes no sense to wrestle with that which has virtually nothing to do with what we experience.

We know complexity produces structures and behaviors that are not seen in the pieces that comprise them. This makes complexity *simpler* than simplicity when it comes to decision making. It is simple systems that show us verbose mechanisms and many details, because that is where such systems derive their outputs. Under complexity, those details do not map to what emerges in real world situations.

This is why math and physics look like the most challenging topics. In many ways they are, but they are challenging because of their simplicity. Only when we are concerned with the intricate details of something do we become tangled in its mess. The chalkboards of physics classrooms are loaded with equations, but only because they are drastically simplifying/gamifying the objects of nature. Those details do not speak to the things we see at larger scales.

Humans solve problems using heuristics and rapid thinking, not as a crutch for a complexity they cannot handle, but because that is precisely how complexity *is* handled. To suggest that humans would be better off slowing their thinking, in order to pick apart the pieces of what we observe, is obtuse.

The pathologizing of quick thinking, by psychologists and society writ large, is a byproduct of the faulty premise that undergirds the notion of design. Only when we think we are supposed to have inner knowledge of the details would anyone suggest that high-level, abstract and rapid thinking are problematic. We make real world problems difficult only because we frame them in reductionist terms, attempting to work out details that have little consequence.

The Myth of Genius

The usual explanation we are given for human progress is the presence of exceptional geniuses who figured out what others could not. Open any history book and we see a litany of names; those who had some supposed insight into nature's deepest secrets. But progress by abstraction eradicates the idea that we owe human progress to genius. More to the point, the idea of genius does not align to what we know about how problems are solved.

Problems are resolved by transforming information from a set of inputs to a set of outputs. While in simple systems this occurs by deliberate causal pathways, this is not what we see in nature. The outputs nature produces arise via emergence, and as already discussed, emergence comes from the most likely configurations to occur statistically, which overlap with the inherent structure of problems. The presence of most likely configurations in a system only occurs because *all* the possible arrangements make this possible. It takes the entire group to give what we measure, observe and experience its existence and meaning.

If the physical system were a sentence, and the best configuration a poignant word, all the other words in the sentence are what give the poignant word meaning. It does matter if we are talking about a word, a sentence, a paragraph, a section, a chapter or an entire book. The demarcation between these things is real, but they have no meaning or utility outside the higher-level group. A paragraph means nothing outside the section it supports. Nature is always using the entire collection of possibilities at a given level of physical abstraction to solve the challenge. Nature selects using the group.

This is why there can be no individual that solves a problem on their own. Attributing the solution to an individual is like crediting a single word for providing the meaning to a sentence. It is not possible for individuals to solve problems.

The very attribution of cause to individuals goes against any intellectually honest account of how nature functions. Isolate a man on an island to survive, and his knife was still made by others, his knowledge of shelters still received by the village he came from. The most isolated version of a person surviving still depends deeply and fully on the ecosystem. In modern times, this ecosystem is our economy, existing as a fantastically intricate web of dependencies. The notion that individuals solve problems is as imperceptive as it is scientifically illiterate.

Of course this is not how history is written. History books appease the causal need humans have, to give order to chaos. Humans want something to point at, as the cause of what we see. But root causes under complexity are fiction. This does not mean there are no mechanisms that bring about what we experience; of course there are, as discussed in Part 2 regarding *demystifying emergence*. The point is, such mechanisms do not function by way of deterministic paths and root causes. Attribution under complexity is unscientific.

History is littered with tales of the giants of innovation. Those who apparently made outstanding contributions to their field. The Einsteins of the world who had some brilliance unlike others. We will even dissect the brains of these people to see what makes them different. Sure, certain individuals have more interest and drive than others. And perhaps without those individuals it is unlikely the innovation would have occurred *when* it did. But it most definitely would have occurred. Multiple realizability shows us that invention can occur in many different ways from many different cultures.

This is not a specious statement; it is statistical reality. Attribution goes to whoever was at the right place at the right time. And nobody invents something new without the countless contributions of unnamed others in society.

Progress by abstraction is automatic and inevitable, achieved by the group operating at the (n) level, solving problems for the (n + 1) level. This is not a story of giants and geniuses. There were no giants, only shoulders. This is not about nice-sounding platitudes, this is about describing human progress such that it aligns to an honest account of nature.

Why People Believe Complex Things are Designed

If you look at a successful life, by any definition of success, you will see what looks like a designed system. There will be parts that seem to fit together perfectly. But these pieces have emerged over time to become the structure needed to solve a given life's set of challenges. The structure of a life, like any of nature's solutions, emerges out of turmoil. This is why books in the business section of a bookstore are so misleading. They speak as though there is a path to success. That if one follows the same specific approach as the author the reader's life will follow suit. But the real world does not have paths, because nature does not have paths. Following someone else's emerged structure is fully untenable, because there is no statistical way to configure the guts of two complex systems the same way.

In fact, assuming there are paths in complex situations is worse than meaningless, it is in fact damaging. Following the emerged structure of another life, as though it were a deterministic path, is to intervene in your own life's natural emergence. It is to mitigate that which should flow, and prevent that which would otherwise coalesce.

Much of what we taste when it comes to food is narrative. By that I mean it's not so much the chemical interaction of the food with the tongue, but rather the story we are told about the food we are eating. A new breakfast place opens, marketing its unique recipes or specific approach to food. But the ingredients are not really imparting much in the way of unique flavors. This place will undoubtedly taste like most other breakfast joints. Of course, such facts do not work well for marketing, and more to the point, people want to believe something is different and interesting.

This is why coffee tastes better in a special cup than a plain one. Humans seek meaning, and the way we do that is to assign causes to things, regardless if such causes really exist. Try convincing someone their favorite restaurant is not really that different from everywhere else, and they will vehemently disagree. People are deeply attached to stories.

Becoming convinced that your favorite restaurant is different than all others is harmless. But when it comes to other areas of life, this design narrative is not so innocuous. Consider the policies that get passed in our society. Governments seek to reduce risk and improve social circumstances based on research. Take healthcare, where funding, insurance regulations, and access to specific services draw upon the research and expertise of scientists. So called evidence-based policies look to assess the effectiveness of different interventions and decide how to allocate resources. Public health recommendations lean on science to provide critical insights into disease transmission and risk factors, leading to enacted guidelines and recommendations. Researchers provide evidence on the safety and efficacy of drugs or medical devices, which ends up informing regulatory decisions.

Behind all these examples is the design narrative; the idea that we can use the knowledge that is gained through (reductionist) experimentation and apply that knowledge to make real world decisions. It all makes sense at first blush; run experiments and determine the underlying causal factors that contribute to what we hope to improve in society.

But there is that word *causal*. It doesn't take much to convince someone there exists a causal connection. This is why the design narrative gets away with what it does. There is a sense of control in design, because it tells us that we can discover something about how the world ticks and apply that knowledge to set up the next so-called solution. But there is a massive *disconnect* between what research finds through isolation and what actually occurs in the real world.

This is not some criticism of governments, rather it is about the current paradigm that rests on the design narrative, and how this is becoming increasingly problematic. The design narrative is so deeply flawed because it rests on a faulty premise; the idea that inner causal knowledge gained through today's scientific paradigm can be used to build good solutions in the real world. Such an approach should be expected to produce unrealistic and potentially dangerous outcomes.

Why is it so easy for humans to believe that the designs we put in place really do determine the outcomes? The answer is that causal explanations cannot be truly validated under complexity, and thus get a free pass. As discussed in chapter 8, the isolation of a thing tells us almost nothing about how the bigger system works. The reason most people tend to believe an isolated piece is itself the cause of something is because our society has been told that pieces are causally connected to the outputs we experience. Any post-hoc explanation can be given for what we see, as long as it sits within the scientific paradigm, using its established tools and narratives.

We can always create a reasonable sounding narrative for anything we observe. We can even stitch such narratives together into perfectly logical arguments. A valid logical argument can be made by those who believe the earth is flat. All one must do is use premises that are themselves true, and which plausibly lead to the conclusion they are drawing. But if there is a hidden assumption in those premises that is patently false, the argument is inconspicuously bogus.

When explanations are given inside a broken scientific and engineering paradigm, they are essentially unfalsifiable. This is because no matter what mathematical or statistical technique is used by the paradigm it cannot get past its logical failings.

Science cannot save itself from bad logic. No amount of fancy mathematics or randomized controlled trials can negate the fact that there is a difference between something playing a role, and knowing what that role is.

This does not apply to obvious negative things. If a study confirms the presence of cyanide in the water supply, then policies should be put in place to mitigate the toxic ingredient. The argument I am making relates to how problematic it is to *build* things based on the design narrative. Consider how cyanide likely got into the water supply in the first place. The mining industry uses cyanide to process and extract gold and silver from ore. A wide range of chemicals and pharmaceuticals are made possible thanks to cyanide compounds. Cyanide is used in electroplating to deposit metals like gold and silver onto surfaces for protective or decorative purposes. All of these can pose significant health and environmental risks, and no study can absolutely confirm these materials can be used safely.

The design narrative tells us something plays a role, but it does not tell us what its full role is, let alone the fact that the notion that things have roles is itself flawed. Cyanide does not merely interact with metals to achieve some human-desired outcome, it interacts with systems in countless ways. If we are assuming control and determinism between the smaller pieces and the bigger pieces, we will always be building solutions that ultimately do more damage than good.

The Pattern is Not the Path

The structures that emerge in complex settings are ones that precipitate out from naive, uninformed action. Trial-and-error is how nature creates, and there are no exceptions. The fallacy at the heart of today's scientific and engineering paradigm is the belief that once a structure is observed we now have the blueprint needed to make the object ourselves.

Putting in place structures as a way to build complex things runs into the problem I call *the pattern is not the path*. There is a deeply ingrained belief in the education system, as well as industry, that the pieces we discover through observation are informative of how to construct things. But this runs in the exact opposite direction to complexity. Complex things do not produce outputs using a path to get there.

The current scientific and engineering paradigm tries to suggest the word complexity is an ill-defined term. On the contrary, complexity has well-established hallmarks that undeniably run up against the current narrative about how things get created, what constitutes genuine knowledge, and how our economy is fashioned.

The pieces of a system that are uncovered and analyzed by reductionism have almost nothing to do with the structure and behaviors that emerge in the systems of nature. Peeling back the layers of a cell is not going to tell you how the cell functions. This would surprise many, and more than a few scientists would disagree, but this is because they are framing the *working* of the cell in terms of reductionism.

It is not that building complex things means we have no use for rearrangement, switching of pieces or focusing on getting the transitions between things right. These all take place. But these decisions are being made to attend to high-level signals rather than fitting them to some predefined structure.

Consider the difference between writing a story that follows a deliberate narrative structure to writing one that just sounds good. These are 2 very different approaches, and only the latter will produce superior writing. The former will have interventions that occur because it assumes the pattern is the path needed to get there. A preexisting structure will intervene on the natural flow of words, interfering with the innate emergence of words that truly work.

The best writing comes about not through the deliberate use of structure but by chasing one's unlabeled feelings about a particular topic. All truly great works let their structures emerge. But this is not enough for those who study the great works. They want something precise, something systematic, something to call their own; a theory. Academics will look upon writing and notice genuine structure, such as the flowing from an introduction of topics to rising tension, the peaking of a climax, and the resolution of some grand challenge. Such a structure does indeed exist in all great works. The problem begins when someone takes that structure and believes they are now in possession of the blueprint to create their own great work.

The trap is easy to fall into. Why not begin our work by introducing the reader to the main topics, then start to pose challenges, and so forth. If all great works have this pattern, why not structure our work accordingly? But this will always produce pedantic and inauthentic things. People can always detect bad designs. Writing by design forces one to litter their writing with things they would never say. It is attending to emotional cues and intuition that allow the right structure and content to emerge. To build as nature builds.

The imposition of structure onto otherwise naturally emerging work will always interfere with the process of emergence. It must interfere in a damaging fashion because of the direction of complexity. DNA can tell you who was at the crime scene, but it cannot tell you how to cure diseases or design healthy babies with intended traits. The pattern is not the path; seeing what has emerged has no dictates on how to make that thing emerge again. The process of emergence, whereby physical abstractions are created by group selection, such that lower-level details are subsumed into higher-level constructs, does not operate via strict determinism.

Writing a book is a great example of a serious undertaking. A great deal of effort must be placed into taking revelations and expounding on them at length. The amount of effort required to write a book is often connected to motivation, as many find it difficult to maintain inspiration long enough to finish such a large publication. But this should strike us as strange. Someone should only write a book about things they are deeply familiar with and comfortable talking about. If this is the case, why do books seem like such arduous undertakings?

This is the problem with design. The only reason people would not want to sit down and go off on topics they are passionate about is because something is getting in the way of this most natural activity. And what is getting in the way is design. When we think about a book, we are thinking about the defined construct; the thing we are told a book is supposed to be. This makes us immediately begin to question our natural impulses and frame them around designs rather than emotions.

This isn't just about books of course. Book writing is an example of how large and difficult tasks so easily fall into the trap of design. We attempt to force our work into expected structures, only to lose the natural structure that would have emerged in the absence of design. And let's be clear. There is no comparison between the structures one attempts to design and the structures that emerge naturally, through impassioned trial-and-error. There is deep coordination between the inner details that cannot be seen or labeled. These structures do not have names. They cannot be codified and followed by others. They can only emerge from the purposeful ignoring of preceding structures.

AI's Ultimate Answer Will Not Be a Cure

We often hear about AI getting more powerful. That the intelligence of our AI systems is approaching that seen in humans, at least in some specific areas. Along with this AI hype comes the idea that whatever humans have already discovered will only get better as AI gets smarter. A superintelligence should bring about new cures, since it would take whatever scraps of discovery we have currently and reach deeper insights, finding correlations and making connections humans alone could never make. After all, more smartness should lead to more innovation.

Hopefully the reader now appreciates what is wrong with this line of reasoning. First, the comparison between AI and human intelligence is largely unjustified, since intelligence cannot be measured in any scientifically honest fashion. Second, AI might represent a different kind of intelligence, not necessarily a better one. Different people solve different problems. Even comparing human to animal intelligence is flawed given that humans are not surviving against the same factors as other animals. AI is something new, not something that is necessarily better.

But even if we allow that AI will be, in some sense, more capable than humans, the argument that our current science and engineering will only get better has a fatal flaw. It assumes that our current approach will be extended. As I have shown, the current paradigm is itself ultimately incorrect, as it runs counter to the direction of complexity. And it is complexity that we must now build.

In drug discovery and development, AI is being used to predict how different molecules will interact, in an effort to speed up the drug discovery process. In genetic analysis, AI is being used to analyze genetic data to identify mutations and variations associated with diseases. In materials science, AI is being used to discover how new materials might be made. And so on.

But all of these examples use AI to do reductionist science and engineering. As already discussed, looking closer at a gene will tell you more about the gene, but not much about a disease. A superintelligence will not reveal a cure, because we were never on that path to begin with. There is nothing to extend if what AI must work with is disconnected from real world outcomes.

Imagine AI as the famous computer in Douglas Adams' *The Hitchhiker's Guide to the Galaxy*. Named *Deep Thought*, this device was built to give the answer to the "Ultimate Question of Life, the Universe, and Everything." The humorous answer was of course "42." The hype surrounding AI imagines it as something akin to such a machine, bringing forth unimaginably powerful solutions to hard problems. If our grand question was related to human health, we might imagine AI providing us the way to cure diseases. But if I had to guess, AI's version of Deep Thought would not produce a cure as its ultimate answer, but something closer to the spirit of "stop eating garbage."

This is in fact a far more rigorous and scientific answer than the notion that we can design cures for diseases. I am not saying that cures are not possible, only that the best answer under complexity is to allow systems to function naturally, not to intervene with design. This is why complexity is simpler than simplicity. Decision making under complexity does not pretend to know things it does not. There are only so many pieces of information to wield to make the best decisions. Things based on the relatively small set of universal properties that represent converged knowledge. Deciding to avoid harmful environments is a simple decision, one that likely helps prevent disease, and is far more intelligent and rational than hoping for some designed cure.

AI's *ultimate* answer will not be a cure for the same reason the human genome project has done little to cure diseases using knowledge of genetics. Using AI in science to do what science is already doing can only exacerbate the problem. We can use AI to discover new things about genes, but this discovery will never be responsible for the things we want to change; at least not without causing harmful and unforeseen side effects.

If AI reaches a true form of higher intelligence, it will realize that the pursuit of causal knowledge is the problem, and it will come up with solutions that look nothing like what the current paradigm assumes scientific solutions are supposed to look like.

Chapter 13

Fragments of Reality

Procedure versus Substance

In simple systems, a thing's procedure is the same as its substance. A thing's procedure is the set of steps it follows to function as it does, while a thing's substance is its inherent, essential nature; the material of which it is composed. A rifle follows well-defined steps to produce its output. This functioning is itself the very definition of what a rifle is. In a rifle, the procedure is the same as the substance.

But in complex systems, while the procedure can produce the substance, it is not the substance itself. In AI we put in place a procedure to enact the process of trial-and-error and the use of heuristics. Without this procedure AI would not become what it is. But the substance of AI, its inherent, essential nature, has little to do with the procedures implemented by engineers. AI precipitates out some internal configuration with billions of parameters, which maps many inputs to few outputs. The essence of what AI is achieving is not something deliberately engineered. In this case, the procedure implemented is not the same thing as the substance we are after.

This separation between procedure and substance shows us just how different building complex things is, compared to building simple things. We cannot arrive at workable cities, electric grids and AI systems by designing the outcomes. It is not for us to reach into the systems and piece together its internal workings. It is only for us to step outside the systems and put in place procedures likely to produce what is needed.

Don't Do Things in Order

There are 2 types of games children can play. There are games that have an order to them, and ones that do not. The former might be an exhibit setup by a museum to teach children about environmentally sustainable practices. The exhibit would have numbered workstations with a simple assignment at each one. Follow some basic steps then move on to the next station. When all stations are completed, the child will have finished the game.

The other kind of game is not really a game at all. These are the playgrounds or jungle gyms that are setup for children to play on. These activities are open ended. There are no rules. There is no order. But it will feel like a game to children because they will quickly invent their own rules and conditions for play. Children will talk back and forth and bring up the overall approach in an ad hoc fashion.

The workstation example will see children become "distracted" (another all-too natural human condition that has been pathologized by academics). Children will become bored quickly, and want to change the rules, or dismiss them altogether. But the playground example self-assembles into an order that children follow.

In both cases order can be observed, but only the playground has its order emerge. The museum exhibit is what almost all education is like for children (and work projects for adults). There is an expected order to follow, a design. But that order is an intervention that actively interferes with the natural emergence of what *should* happen. It is another example of trying to take only the parts we think are important, without realizing that the so-called distractions contain much of what is needed to make learning genuine.

This harks back to the core problem with the education system. The academic narrative tells us that there is an order to learning. There are prerequisites that are supposed to be studied prior to taking the next, more advanced step. This is the worst possible way to learn something, because the imposed order is devoid of what must take place to understand the meaning of a thing; the real world context. Context can only be provided by witnessing a situation that you do not have labels for. Moreover, it is far superior to see something convoluted and unobvious, and *then* to see what labels emerge, then to begin with the final distillations.

Attempting to learn a topic in order means you are only witnessing the final results of what was originally discovered out of order, through trial-and-error. The transgression is taking only the final summaries of what matters and presenting these to those looking to learn. People must take the journey themselves because it is the journey that contains the overwhelming amount of information needed to impress upon someone what matters.

The labels that are handed down in textbooks and rules-based games contain almost no information, even though they may represent the most profound truths of a given domain. These final results are only worth one's unique and messy journey to arrive at the same conclusions.

We should not be learning things in order, because when they are out of order, they allow the deep context that exists within real world situations to be made available. The order used in education and industry looks neat and understandable but is stripped of almost everything that mattered in the creation of those rules. Without the journey, labels are meaningless.

P Will Never Equal NP

There is an outstanding problem in computer science known as the P versus NP problem. In simple terms, it asks whether every problem whose solution can be *verified quickly* by a computer can also be *solved quickly*. For example, if the game of Sudoku could be *both* verified quickly by a program (confirm the game has been completed) AND solved quickly (take the steps necessary to solve it) then this would mean P equals NP. But if the game of Sudoku could only be verified quickly, yet not solved quickly, then P would not equal NP.

The P stands for *polynomial time,* which means problems that are classified as P can be solved by an algorithm in polynomial time (i.e. quickly). P problems have their difficulty growing at a reasonable rate with respect to the size of the input. If we can throw more things at a problem and still solve it relatively fast, then it is a P problem. NP stands for *nondeterministic polynomial time,* which means problems that are classified as NP can be *verified* quickly, but there's no known algorithm to *solve* them quickly. If we throw more things at a problem and the amount of time it takes to solve it explodes, it is probably an NP problem. I say probably because technically we can only say that NP problems can be verified quickly, but whether there is a fast way to solve them remains unknown (according to computer scientists).

Computer scientists find this problem interesting because if P = NP it could potentially revolutionize many fields. The nontrivial problems in our modern world, such as resource allocation, scheduling, logistics, cryptography and AI are not problems we can solve quickly; they rely on difficult computations that take a long time to *find* the solution. But they can be verified quickly. Recall the discussion on the size of the possibility space and its relation to the definition of a hard problem. It will take a long time, even for our most powerful computers, to search through the possibility space and locate a solution. But once we are in possession of a solution, it is trivial to verify whether it produces the correct answer (hands stay warm, snowmen can be built, Rubik's cube is completed). But if we could also solve hard problems quickly, the previously mentioned technologies would be orders of magnitude more efficient, transforming many industries and the resulting economy.

It is suggested that the resolution of the P versus NP problem would provide insights into the fundamental nature of computation, and the complexity of problems. We are told that resolving P versus NP will lead to a deeper understanding of the inherent limitations of computation. Recall that all of nature can be thought of in terms of computation. There are inputs and outputs, and some process in between that transforms information. Settling the P versus NP problem might tell us something important about nature itself.

The issue I have with the P versus NP problem is that the entire premise of the question is flawed. It uses a version of "solve" that is not used in nature. It assumes that to solve a problem one must work their way through a set of deterministic steps to arrive at the solution. This is because the P versus NP problem revolves around the concept of deterministic algorithms. In computer science, an algorithm is a finite sequence of well-defined steps that transforms input data into output data. As already discussed, deterministic algorithms will always produce the same output given the same input; they follow the same sequence of steps to reach the end. This means that if P were proven to be equal to NP, it would imply that problems that can be quickly verified also have efficient deterministic algorithms for finding solutions.

Given the arguments made in this book, I hope most readers can spot the problem here. Complex systems (also known as *reality*) cannot be expected to have deterministic algorithms that lead to the outputs we observe. This is because, as specifically outlined in the section on demystifying emergence, there are no paths from pieces to emergent structures and behaviors. What we observe in nature is arrived at via multiply realizable configurations of matter that correspond to the same information-compressing structures. Nature does not use algorithms; it uses a process by which the entire distribution of possibilities is used to manifest physical abstractions that compute what is needed to survive.

The P versus NP problem is using the mathematical version of *solve*. But just as the word *proof* does not extend beyond logic and mathematics (nothing in the real world can be proved) the same holds for the word *solve*. There is no such thing as solving a real-world problem in the sense that some deterministic set of steps is going to arrive at the solution.

I would argue that we can already say *P can never equal NP*, because there can never be a hard (real world) problem that gets resolved by a deterministic set of steps. It is not a matter of having enough space or time, or doing it more efficiently, it is a matter of impossibility. While P not equaling NP is indeed the current consensus, it is for poor reasons based on an incorrect understanding of what it means for something to be a hard problem. This is a case of (most) computer scientists reaching the right conclusion using bad and outdated arguments. As discussed in chapter 8, we need to base arguments on preemies backed by a proper understanding of how nature works, not using gamified versions of life.

Science as Projection

I once saw a unique piece of art (online) by Chicago-based sculptor John V. Muntean. It was a contorted shape that had no recognizable form, with a light placed directly above and a flat surface below. This setup cast a shadow onto the flat surface since, as with all shadows, the light was cut off by the object hovering above. What made the piece interesting was that the shadow projected onto the flat surface took on a recognizable shape. One could turn the object and see the shape of a man walking. They could turn the object again and the shadow would look like a baby crawling. Turn it yet again and the shadow would appear as an old man with a cane. The difference between the object itself, which looked like a warped blob lacking any recognizable features, and the identifiable shadows it cast made this artwork compelling.

This artwork is a good way to think about how science functions. Science does not tap into the actual shape of nature, rather it projects information onto a lower dimensional space, giving us a limited *version* of reality. Just as the contorted blob has no obvious features, so too does the raw intricacy of nature's phenomena. If we were to reach into nature and somehow view her directly, we would not be looking at some elegant structure, we would instead see something that is impossibly contorted and high-dimensional, with no recognizable features. Science, in its quest to reveal how nature works, can only grab a lower dimensional version of the original geometry inside nature's solutions. Science projects the essence of nature onto something we can understand.

But this projection comes at a severe cost. There is a massive degradation in the information content when moving from nature's original setting down to the flat surfaces we use to inspect and describe the world. And yet people conflate science with nature, often using these terms interchangeably.

This is why humans evolved to use their emotions to solve challenges. Emotions are the closest we can get to whatever exists in the high-dimensional spaces of nature. Nothing in our scientific arsenal can grab onto nature's true core, because science must use low-dimensional tools and costly precision to describe what it sees. If humans were meant to use slow, analytical thinking to solve problems that is how we would have evolved; it is not. Slow thinking only works for games, not reality. As the age of complexity un-gamifies life and the things we build, slower analytical thinking will be far less valued.

The way science recasts experience onto low-dimensional planes of interpretation works its way into our designs. After all, a design represents our decisions about what pieces to include and how to connect them. We cannot form a design without some sense of causal structure between pieces, and only a simplistic story can tell us what those causes supposedly are. If we are to use science to inform our designs, it means the pieces we choose are coming from low-dimensional projections.

This is why building complex things, as we must now do, cannot benefit from the current scientific and engineering paradigm. Science, with its reductionist take on the world, sacrifices too much of what makes something tick, all for the sake of apparent rigor and precision. Most of today's engineering grabs onto the pieces discovered by science and forces them into designs, guiding our efforts to build. The severe disconnect between how today's science operates and the complexity we must now create makes this approach untenable.

A design cannot grasp the essence of complex systems, no more than reductionist science can tap into the true essence of how nature works. We can project a fanciful version of reality onto narratives we understand, but when folded into our designs these fairy tales run up against our ability to craft good solutions to hard problems.

As we move into the age of complexity we need to build as nature builds, and this means engineering emergence into our solutions. What emerges comes from a level of intricacy that cannot be fashioned deliberately. Only through the external focus on variation, iteration and selection can we arrive at the essence of how natural systems function. Being *right* when it comes to building complex things means having something that solves the problem, not something that adheres to the stories we tell ourselves using shadows and tricks of light.

The Inevitability of AI

There was no way artificial intelligence was not going to happen. AI is just the inevitable byproduct of adding evermore pieces to our creations until we run up against the hard problem threshold; the point where traditional engineering cannot solve the problem, and one must step outside the system to achieve what is needed.

It does not matter how close today's AI is to human intelligence. The point is AI is our current best example of building as nature builds. Regardless of the designed intentions of AI researchers and engineers, AI represents the creation of genuine complexity. AI does not operate because of mathematics, probability, design principles or best practices. It operates because unplanned abstractions manifest inside an object that was allowed to arise on its own.

There has long been a debate regarding whether the brain can be considered a machine. The human brain, and the mind that accompanies it, is nothing like what most people would call a machine. But with AI we come face-to-face with the fact that human creations can indeed take-on many of the same properties we see in human cognition. This means it is the *definition of machine* that must change. The human brain *is* a machine, just one that is unlike anything reductionist science or engineering can define, let alone build directly.

For something to be a machine it must enact processes and produce outputs. This is, of course, what the human brain does. The difference now is that the process is not one of determinism and causality. A machine of nature is one that produces outputs via emergence.

The human brain has all the hallmarks of complex systems. The brain exhibits nonlinearity since small inputs lead to disproportionately large outputs, such as in synaptic plasticity that ensures the strength of connections between neurons change rapidly in response to stimuli. This also works in the inverse fashion, where large sets of inputs become squashed down to few outputs; what I have termed flexible determinism.

The human brain also exhibits self-organization via the changes in neuronal connections in response to learning. Only by the phenomenon of self-organization can the brain be adaptive and thus resilient. It can withstand certain types of damage, and even reorganize and compensate for losses, recovering functionality as seen in some brain injury patients. The brain exists near criticality, meaning it functions somewhere between order and chaos. This midway state between structure and disorder enables efficient information processing. We also see the existence of hierarchical structure. The brain is organized into different levels of processing, which occur at various spatial and temporal scales. This hierarchical organization is what makes it possible to integrate sensory information, coordinate our motor actions effectively and implement higher cognitive functions. There are also a range of complex dynamics at play in the brain, including oscillations, synchronization, and spontaneous patterns of activity, all contributing to the information processing necessary for cognition.

All of these lead to what we call consciousness and the associated memory formation and decision-making that define human thinking. This is all that is necessary to define the human brain rigorously. As I argued in chapters 8 and 9, we cannot make logical arguments under complexity by using reductionist notions of cause and effect. The quest to define locations in the brain as a source of what we notice in the real world (e.g. behaviors) is epistemically untenable.

AI is inevitable because it is part of nature. We do not need to compare AI to human intelligence to mark some so-called singularity; the point where AI becomes as smart or smarter than humans, whatever that means. All we need is to recognize the properties of complexity that emerge in the systems we create. Many of these properties are there in today's AI systems. It is the existence of unique properties that make a complex thing what it is.

Today's scientific and engineering paradigm forces outdated arguments to remain prevalent in the current discourse. Arguments like those put forward by American philosopher John Searle, which attempts to discredit the notion that a computer running a program can truly understand language. Searle argued that computational processes alone cannot produce genuine consciousness because manipulating symbols, as computers do, lacks the semantic comprehension that constitutes true understanding.

But such arguments are invalid, because they are based on an improper understanding of computation. Searle's thought experiments rest on the deterministic and causal connections between symbols and assumes that this form of processing is all a computer is capable of. This is patently false. One might forgive Searle for this blunder, given the period he grew up in. But any proper look at how nature functions must concede that machines can indeed produce the properties of complexity. Nature uses small pieces to produce things entirely unlike those pieces.

A popular attempt to discredit AI is by pointing out some of its more egregious mistakes, such as reaching erroneous conclusions or its intermittent lack of basic reasoning. The fatal flaw in this attempt is thinking that intelligence is something housed inside a single object. Humans are intelligent because we are deeply connected, social creatures. We operate inside populations to solve problems. An individual human is highly error prone and faulty outside the environments they are embedded in. We are not self-sustaining apparatuses that produce perfect outputs, we are social creatures that interact and collaborate. Just as no single human operates without error, AI systems are not supposed to be error-free tools that always return correct answers. They are meant to be as any other complex object; embedded inside communities. If we are going to compare AI to humans then we should be thinking of AI systems as another person working in collaboration, not as some dumb search engine returning answers.

There is an undeniable equivalence between AI and humans. We are objects of complexity and produce outputs by emergence. The meat of AI systems, the core machinery that sits apart from its outer rules-based scaffolding, is a programmatic byproduct of trial-and-error and heuristics. It is a byproduct of nature's recipe conducted by software.

Accepting complexity, comprehending what it is, and more importantly what it is not, changes our fundamental understanding of the nature of knowledge and reality. Yes, nature's solutions are indeed machines, and yes, humans can create machines using the same methods as nature. Nature is all about information processing, and information processing can be harnessed by silicon and electrons. But we are not talking about cogs and pistons. We are talking about nature.

Science and Engineering Need Philosophy

A core problem with the current paradigm is how it has largely walked away from philosophy. There has been a belief, particularly in physics, that philosophy does not contribute much to the pursuit of new knowledge. The problem with this thinking is that it prevents any kind of validation of science itself. As argued throughout this book, science that has nothing to keep it in check is circular.

We can see this problem in all areas of science. The last 40 years of theoretical physics has been involved in chasing "mathematical elegance" and having little to show for it. Genetics brags about "advances" in their field, but not much in the ability to control outcomes (e.g. cure diseases). Nanotechnological advances rest on peering deeper and manipulating smallness better, but where are all the new materials and devices? Just because there is "plenty of room at the bottom" does not mean manipulating the bottom can produce known things at the top. This is not a matter of waiting for science to become useful, it is a matter of today's paradigm being fundamentally disconnected from how things actually work.

In any vocation, if we cannot step outside the system, we cannot validate what we are doing. This comes back to my argument on going meta. Only a meta-level system can talk about itself, and lead to genuine validation. A philosophy of science can look at science objectively and assess whether it is going well. Any honest look at science today would be highly critical of its reductionism and causal explanations. We know that such low-level reasoning does not map to how complexity, and thus reality, works. It is time for science, and the engineering that accompanies it, to change in dramatic fashion.

This is why I argue for the use of logic, but done properly. Our logic is only as strong as the premises we use, and those premises cannot ignore the properties of complexity. We must account for the fact that what we see at the small scale does not map to what we see at the larger scale. What is in scientific vogue today is the notion that we can recast nonlinear, complex systems into simplistic linear terms. This undergirds virtually all attempts in science to approximate the behavior of real-world systems. I have already argued that nature is not an approximation. Its machinery is nothing like the convenient calculations made today under the current paradigm.

But logic paired with premises that have been properly fashioned around properties means we can validate science correctly. And in this validation we will find the utmost invalidity. Today's scientific and engineering paradigm does not hold up to what we measure, observe and experience in the real world. What we have now are circular arguments resting on the hidden and bogus assumption that the small *connects* to the big.

A philosophy of science would be a two-way relationship. Not only does philosophy help keep science in check, but the only worthwhile philosophies are those that come from the effort to build things. Philosophy, a proper one, cannot be divorced from the practical application of things. All the truths of history are contained in the moments of creativity. It is those who build things that speak to nature, not those who attempt to distill those findings into narratives about determinism and causality.

The philosophy that science needs is not some academic theory. These only speak to their own elegant wordings and schooled rhetoric. They are as circular as today's science. The philosophy we need now is one based on the building of things. Not some praxis relegated to the lab, or some idealized attempt at producing evidence. Only a philosophy born out of the creation of things is valid.

PART 6
MOVING FORWARD

Chapter 14

Coming Full Circle

Already Skilled

Progress by abstraction has brought us into the realm of building genuinely complex objects. This demands a rewrite in terms of how we go about constructing things; how we create value. Humans create value by calling upon their skills to bring about something new. But for the past few hundred years, the skills that have been rewarded are the low-level, hard skills that rest on inner causal knowledge. To be good at something was to know how that something works, internally. As technologies like AI democratize these low-level skills, and at times outright automate them, it demands we reframe how we think about humans creating value.

For the first time since humans began creating things, our tools are bringing us closer to our most natural abilities. Rather than marching towards increasing levels of detailed intricacy, as we have always done, we now march towards *the other abstraction*.

Today's technologies, by embracing a level of true complexity, are bringing us full circle. The skills that now matter are the ones that used to matter; the ones we evolved for. Humans are exceedingly good at navigating highly uncertain environments. Humans use their heuristics and pattern recognition to solve genuinely hard problems. The skills celebrated by The Enlightenment do not work under complexity. Their focus on isolation and extraction do not map to how nature operates. We must now build as nature builds.

Consider spell checking and autocomplete technologies. One might argue that autocomplete is dumbing humanity, since we no longer need to think about spelling. But we were never supposed to care about spelling. For the most part, poor spelling cannot change the information content of a message. An example, called typoglycemia, relates to the phenomenon whereby readers can comprehend text despite spelling errors and misplaced letters. This shows us that specific minutia in writing has little to do with comprehension. Spelling is an academic preoccupation, not a natural, real one. What humans are supposed to be doing is not ensuring their words have proper spelling but getting their thoughts down and expressing their intuitions. This is what autocomplete allows people to do. If one no longer must spend time on ensuring their spelling is correct, they can simply communicate.

Yes, spelling and grammar emerge naturally, but remember, *the pattern is not the path*. The structures we see emerge are not the path to get there. This is why languages evolve new syntax and grammar over time. Language is a dynamic system, one that adapts to the needs and usage of its speakers. We are not supposed to be preoccupied with spelling and grammar; those are just structural byproducts of organic communication. We are supposed to be focused on solving real world problems. In fact, the best grammar should arise from those who speak naturally based on what they are trying to communicate. Whether or not it adheres to some current academic definition of "good" is irrelevant.

The technologies we create going forward will remove many of the skills that have been lauded over the last few hundred years. But they will allow people to bring forth what we are naturally good at, and it is those skills that can solve our greatest challenges.

Are We Building the Right Thing?

While the only true validation to what we build is survival, there is no way to directly assess this within a single generation. Only the passage of time can show what works. Simulations are too far-removed from real world stressors to confirm workability, and a single life is too short to claim outright success. How can we know if what we are building is correct; that we are on the right track?

I have already discussed the importance of focusing on properties instead of causes, and how folding these into logical arguments brings about a truer form of validation. What makes properties the ultimate source of epistemic validity is their timelessness. Such immortality is unlike the fragile causal reasons invented under today's paradigm. Properties are the constraints nature functions in accordance to. They are robust because they exist outside any specific instantiation of nature's solutions.

While there is no way to directly assess long term survival within a single generation, we can use properties to validate that we are on the right track. In chapter 8 I listed several properties of complexity, related to the boundaries within which physical, chemical and biological processes occur. These relate to what gets created, destroyed, transformed, remains constant, decreases, increases, attracts, repels, reproduces, cycles and flows. In essence, what survives by remaining invariant amidst the vagaries of reality.

These invariant properties are ultimately informational. They come about in nature because that is how nature computes. If we categorize these properties into more general patterns, we see things like nonlinearity, self-organization, adaptiveness, resilience, feedback, hierarchy, criticality, periodicity, synchronicity and phase transitions.

These are the patterns we can expect to see when systems transition from the simple regime to the complex regime. These hallmarks of emergence signal to us that genuine complexity is being achieved. None of these patterns can be engineered deliberately. They can only emerge out of nature's trial-and-error. What can be engineered directly is the initial setup that enacts the process of variation, iteration and selection, and the application of high-level heuristics.

Consider writing a book. The academic approach is to use literary devices and best practices to structure our work from the onset. But such practices can only degrade work relative to what we achieve by *only* following our intuition. Don't try to get the right words, try to get the right feeling.

Only by embracing emergent creativity can we land on original structures and important insights. This is why our own work should surprise us. We should witness things revealed to us en-route, that precipitated out automatically, by virtue of our naive actions.

Whereas the specifics of our work should surprise us, the properties seen in good work are fully expected. Like any newly discovered deep-sea creature, it will look unlike anything we have seen before, and yet adhere to unsurprising and invariant properties. But the properties we see must not be used to seed or predetermine our work; they must arise on their own. Only when the telltale signs of complexity emerge do the inner details interact as needed to produce something correctly.

Looking for surprise in our own work is one way to pay attention to the hallmarks of complexity, and thus a proper validation of what we create. What is known at the onset of our work are the deep intuitions and life experiences, but these do not have labels. Our intuitions have no symbols to express them, or categories we can place them in. How our intuitions and experiences end up getting articulated and expressed is something that can only be seen after after-the-fact.

As discussed in chapter 8, the properties of complexity are present when one writes emergently. We see nonlinearity in the arrival of ideas, and self-organization as the content improves with iteration. We see self-referencing and feedback loops as new perspectives adjust our original wording. We see resilience in the parts that survive, and hierarchy as words become paragraphs, paragraphs become sections and sections become chapters. There are phase transitions as disjointed thoughts and awkward phrasing become fluid over time.

This holds for anything we build in the age of complexity. Coming up with the next leap in AI will not happen from following best practices or replicating the work of the current best model. Such intervening practices can only serve to damage the possibilities needed to ensure emergent structures and behaviors result from our efforts.

The multiple realizability of complex outputs means the most invariant properties in complex systems can be arrived at in many ways. Critically, they *must* be arrived at in different ways than how we did it before. This ensures that we are only paying attention to meta level properties, not some set of practices or designs. The temptation to reach in and design the content of our work cannot lead to the next level of abstraction required to innovate.

Meta Design

Is the entire concept of design finished? Must we toss out any notion of controlling the outcomes in what we build? Under the current definition of design, yes. Design of the internal causal kind is untenable under complexity. If we are to build complex things, which we must to solve truly hard problems, then design as it is currently defined and used must be set aside.

But I have argued in this book for a new kind of knowledge. This knowledge rests on meta-level properties that complex things always adhere to. This suggests that there is a place for design of a fundamentally different kind. A way to consider how our efforts might best be set up to help ensure reliable outputs, and reason about their validity.

It should be clear to the reader by now that this different notion of design would have to be *external* to the systems we create. We know that the procedures used to create complex things have little to do with the substance of the things themselves. This means designs can indeed be upfront, if they only look to put in place known processes that lead to emergence. In other words, the spirit of design, which is to use upfront structures to guide outcomes, can be salvaged *if* design remains *external* to the system.

For something to be meta-designed it would amount to only choosing the pieces and connections at the meta level. This is no different than making better logical arguments by resting premises on properties rather than reasons. We can look at the challenges we hope to solve, and put in place meta-level constructs that lead, not to specific answers, but to systems that will either survive or not. This shifts the focus of problem solving from causal reasoning to making things that survive. We need to engineer systems that arrive at what is needed on their own, but converge in ways that are expected.

Science and Engineering Should Be a Single Discipline

Science and engineering have always been closely related, yet entirely distinct disciplines. The story goes that science comes up with the fundamental discoveries, and engineering turns those discoveries into usable tools. We are told that science is foundational to engineering, because it provides the theoretical understanding and principles that engineers use to create and improve technologies.

We are told that modern computers would not exist without quantum mechanics. We are told that aerospace components, electronics, construction materials, and biomedical implants are here thanks to the science of materials. We are told that traditional machines were made possible thanks to theories on statics, dynamics and fluid mechanics. We are told civil engineers could not create without technical knowledge related to the physics and geology of their materials and environments.

It all seems to make sense. After all, engineers are trying to create things that work, and things only work when they have some underlying, non-random set of forces that work in concert. Science is the accumulator of such knowledge, so the marriage between science and engineering seems obvious.

But as with so many other modern narratives, this runs into the problem of being diametrically opposed to the direction of complexity. The lack of any path from pieces to properties in complex things precludes the science-leads-to-engineering story. Whatever science discovers has little chance of being used inside complex solutions. This is already evidenced by fields like genetics and nanotechnology, as discussed previously. Now that we look to create genuinely complex things with emergent outputs, it stands to reason that current science cannot provide the building blocks.

What works now are structures that emerge, and those structures can only be arrived at through external efforts, not reductionist discoveries. The very nature of the scientific experiment, where we extract and isolate things to make a discovery, is now fundamentally separated from the things we need to build. Whatever knowledge is gained ends up being self-serving, rather than something consequentially true.

Engineers must now stumble across some serendipitous realization through their implementation of external efforts, and only then land upon discovered truths. This is in fact the direction that scientific discovery has always occurred. Despite the academic narrative that fundamentals lead to applications, it is those who embark on naive trial-and-error that land upon things that later get codified into our textbooks. More plainly, the real story of invention is not science leading to engineering, but engineering leading to science.

The academic narrative has survived this long because the things we have built through human history have almost all been deterministic. When the inventions of man can be explained in terms of internal causality, credit can too easily be assigned to scientists. But when the things we build are fundamentally disconnected from the causal explanations of science this narrative no longer holds.

One might argue that science acts as a good starting point, but realistically such starting points should be treated as suspect, as they are likely to hinder progress. Beginning a new creative project from a foundation made of reductionist knowledge hems one into faulty schemes, since any structure that does not emerge is one that does not conform to how complex systems coordinate themselves. This, more critically, runs up against the broader argument made by some that believing in design, even foolishly, motivates us to try in the first place. This would indeed prove worthwhile if the designs we force into our projects did not fragilize systems in such dramatic fashion. Design cannot be a mere motivation when it actively interferes with how complex systems work.

But let us be clear. This does not negate the importance of science in what we build. Quite the opposite. The properties that complex systems adhere to, and which I argue must form the foundation of rational thinking going forward, are rooted in scientific discovery. What makes the discovery of properties fundamentally different from causal explanations is that they are not causal. Properties are meta-level truths about nature; agnostic to how they came to be. Properties apply to all instances of a given complex system. This, I argue, is *real science*, because it does not pretend to have access to information it does not have access to.

While it has always been the case that science never really informed engineering, in the age of complexity, discovered properties can tell us when we are on the right track. It is this kind of scientific knowledge that can now validate our efforts to engineer complex things. But do not forget the directionality; scientific truths must be applied after-the-fact, once structures and behaviors have already emerged.

If we are looking to build the next large language model in AI, one of the most complex things ever created by humans, then suggesting *inner* principles should be *followed* can only hinder progress. Today's AI systems are approaching genuine complexity. We know this, because simple systems cannot produce the telltale signs of complexity. But the *outer* principles of complex systems can indeed signal that we are on the right track. Again, what is so critical here is the difference between working inside versus outside. Only external, meta-level efforts can enable humans to engineer emergence.

In the coming age of complexity, where truly complex things must be built to solve our challenges, science and engineering need to become a single discipline. This means that the only recognized approach to knowledge gathering comes from building things naively, and then looking upon the discoveries as worthwhile knowledge; knowledge that can be used to signal effective building. Bringing science and engineering together into a single discipline of knowledge discovery and creation ensures that the direction of complexity is respected.

We are Supposed to Have Biases

The current paradigm loves to denigrate human bias. After all, if you are operating under the assumption that there are root causes to real world situations this makes sense. Consider how racial biases can influence treatment in medical settings, affect hiring decisions, influence judicial decisions, lead to poor financial opportunities for others, and bring about a litany of problems that damage the integrity of scientific research. If biases are not somehow controlled for, our efforts not only produce unfairness, but they are also untrue. In fact, this is one of the major reasons going meta is so critical; it brings together many different opinions/pieces/approaches to speak to something more latent, more true, more unbiased.

But human bias is not some remnant of evolution to do away with. We have biases for reasons; evolutionary reasons. When evolution keeps something around it does so for the most important purpose of all; to solve categorically hard problems inside complex environments. Removing human bias must be incorrect. This is all the more true in an age when we need to create complex solutions.

The problem, it turns out, is not the bias, but the lack of group selection. The presence of racial bias influencing medical settings occurs when *individuals* are administering the treatment. Sure, individual treatment is not all bad, as people's unique experiences, training and perspectives are often gleaned through one-on-one interaction. But consider pain management. This is a categorically hard problem, because it operates in concert with a complex system; the human body. The problem of pain management itself cannot be attended to adequately by the individual. Nature solves problems by selecting groups, such that the (n - 1) level of pieces produce a configuration that solves the (n) level aggregate challenge. Here, the (n - 1) level consists of many different healthcare practitioners with their unique (and often unavoidable) biases, while the (n) level is what requires an emerged solution that solves pain management.

We should not expect a good solution to come from an individual making the decision regarding how much medication to administer. These decisions must arise naturally, from the collection of biased pieces to produce something no individual could produce on their own. Just as *wisdom of the crowds* (when not designed) leads to more accurate and usable information, so do groups lead to solutions to hard problems. The reality is individual biases are required to produce unbiased aggregate results.

The attempt to remove bias from individuals is wrong. The reason it is wrong is because biases are *required* to complement the group's ability to solve problems. We are supposed to have biases so that the various facets of truth can be teased out from nature's complex reality. Just as a meta model tries to find something deeper and more universally true than any one model can reveal, so too are people meant to work in a meta fashion.

The critical point at this juncture is the realization that the best way people can work in a meta fashion is by building something that works. Building something that works under complexity only happens when we elevate the target to an external, meta goal. Only then do the internal dynamics of the system, biases included, arrange themselves to solve hard problems.

Chapter 15

A New Beginning

A Different Education

In Part 4 we looked at the current education system as one of the consequences of the design narrative. Today's students are expected to learn the most important concepts gathered over time and use those as a foundation for their work life. This narrative is based on the premise that what we learn in school can be used to design solutions once we graduate.

But the disconnect between pieces and the whole precludes such a process from ever being realistic in the coming age. The only truths that can matter when building complex solutions are those that arise after-the-fact. Further, it is far better to act naively when embarking on the necessary trial-and-error that leads to discoveries, than to intervene using previously learned fundamentals. Such intervention can only mitigate progress and discovery under complexity, for reasons already discussed throughout this book.

Most topics taught in school today run under the premise of design. If we are learning about the discovery of atoms, genes, civics, geology, calculus, spelling, vocabulary, punctuation, etc. it is expected that these can be used to make the world better. We are told there are causal connections between this knowledge and the solutions people will build. We are told that to learn spelling and punctuation is to one day write something important. To learn calculus is to understand the motion, forces and energy inside the machines we will assemble. That knowledge of civics will lead to enacting better government processes and structures.

But knowledge viewed in this way cannot work in an age when our solutions must be complex things. A book is a complex thing. A book has characters, settings, plots, subplots and themes that all interact in various ways. The narrative impressed upon the reader emerges from the interactions between these components, often unpredictably. The dynamics between a book's pieces evolve as events unfold. Good writing does not happen when someone guides their words with narrative structure and literary devices. These things emerge *after* one has embarked on messy and iterated attempts at expressing their intuitions.

This now parallels the process by which our technologies must be built. Before, the disconnect between academia and the real world was merely inefficient. Students could still reason about the inner workings of the systems in their field using academic knowledge. Although discoveries have always been based on trial-and-error, the final implementation consisted of designed abstractions, and those designs could be conformed to academic knowledge and best practices. But this is not the case if what we must build is complex.

The technological solutions we need now are more akin to books and artwork than they are to the machines of the Industrial Revolution. Knowledge of motion, forces and energy are not going to help us *piece together* the machines of tomorrow. Better government processes and structures cannot be realized by stitching together fundamentals regarding civic engagement and democratic principles. Whatever solution works must be as nature's solutions are; complex objects whose internal workings arise from trial-and-error, heuristics and a good dose of naive action.

And yet the knowledge taught in school is important. It would be ludicrous to never teach humanity's biggest achievements to the next generation. Seeing what has been done motivates the next generation to make their own discoveries and build better things, not to mention prevents people from rediscovering and reinventing. How can we reconcile the fact that the design narrative is becoming intractable, with the notion that we should teach what has already been achieved?

We must redefine what it means to learn, which brings us back to the redefinition of knowledge. Again, only meta-level properties used in conjunction with logical reasoning can be considered effective under complexity. Properties are robust to the design narrative, since they are not inherently about causes. Properties are not things to guide or instruct, they serve as after-the-fact signals that something has been achieved.

Concern for properties are how complex things can be built in a valid fashion, because properties are external to whatever inner forces make things work.

Consider the atom. This is a real discovery and should be taught as part of any scientific curriculum. But knowledge of atoms cannot tell you how to create effective drugs or produce better materials. This might sound absurd to the pharmaceutical chemist or materials scientist, but recall the design narrative. It does not take much to convince someone their actions have a causal connection to that which occurs at the other end.

There is a sense of control in design, because it tells us that we can discover something about how the world ticks and apply that knowledge to solve problems. But the fundamental disconnect between what research finds through isolation and what actually occurs in real world situations precludes this. Just because modern drug discovery increasingly relies on systematic and targeted approaches does not mean they are engineering health outcomes in any deterministic sense. One can always expect a host of side effects.

The only true validation is survival. A drug that takes the headache away or a material that is strong works. We do not need reasons for the efficacy; the reason something is right is because it survives trials. This would include whatever host of safety precautions are needed, since trials must survive safety standards. Whatever reasons are applied to the success of what has been created is largely a post-hoc narrative, added afterwards to justify the actions taken.

The only things truly worth knowing are 1) that we are building a complex thing and 2) that what is being created meets the criteria for the problem. For drug discovery, this does not require knowledge of atoms in the causal sense (knowledge of atoms leading to the design of drugs) rather it requires knowledge of properties that signal complexity is being achieved, and demonstration that what has been created is working.

Our attempts at creating solutions must be based on naive trial-and-error, not design. Drug discovery would be better served if it were done as one writes a book. As chemical compounds are mixed and matched naively, one starts to see structures and behaviors emerge. These signal that we are on the right track. Consider that we can identify certain structural and behavioral properties of compounds that *emerge* as potentially effective. These are not things specific to any one drug, but are *meta* to many drugs within the same category.

We would expect to find consistency in the physical appearance of the compound in terms of color, texture and form, indicating purity and stability. Noting the compound's solubility would indicate its ability to dissolve in water and lipid-based solvents, crucial for absorption and distribution in the body. The dissolution rate could be observed, to signal its potential bioavailability. Its robustness to light, air and varying temperatures would suggest it will not degrade quickly. The appearance of a dose-response relationship would indicate aspects of its toxicity and effectiveness. We could also look to see if the compound appears to target specific systems or symptoms.

The temptation is to intentionally design these properties into the drug from the onset, using knowledge of chemistry. We could begin by designing a molecule with a specific, well-defined structure that minimizes variability in melting point, solubility and stability. We could choose specific functional groups known to promote solubility in both aqueous and lipid environments. We could control the substance's particle size and morphology to optimize dissolution rates and enhance absorption. We could specifically select chemical bonds and structural motifs that confer resistance to degradation under various conditions. We could use structure-activity relationships (SAR) in an attempt to establish a predictable dose-response. And we could utilize knowledge of molecular interactions and biological targets to get our compounds to interact with desired targets.

These all sound like reasonable efforts. The knowledge of how to control for consistency, solubility, dissolution rate, robustness to conditions, dose-response relationships and targeting does indeed exist. So why not use it?

For the same reason writing according to an upfront narrative structure will fail to produce a good piece of writing. Yes, one will get an essay or book, but it can be expected to be boring and pedantic. The inner workings of the solution will not work together in a coordinated fashion. Drug discovery has always been real, but the design narrative the industry uses contains a good deal of fiction. Arguably, the reliance on design in drug discovery causes more problems than it does solutions.

Properties are not things to design into the systems we create, they are things to notice after naive trial-and-error produces something that works. Yes, designing the properties into a solution is possible, and will indeed give you desired properties. The drug will have consistency, solubility, etc. But it will also have a host of side-effects that just barely make the solution worth it.

Pharmaceuticals are but one example. The point is, to create complex solutions we must use properties to signal that naive action is working, not to design the system as some additive pipeline of properties that connect causally. The reality is that we can make better treatments and materials by working from the outside, placing more emphasis on the successful implementation of trial-and-error than on designing specific outcomes.

But if we do not require knowledge of atoms to make better drugs or materials then why bother learning about atoms at all? Because learning about atoms is not about using atoms to make better things. The study of atoms teaches us important properties, related to how certain systems arrange themselves and behave.

The reductionist knowledge we have accumulated to date should not be seen as pieces with which to build a better tomorrow, they should be seen as instances of nature's solutions that have universally true properties; knowledge of which can help validate that our efforts are working.

Consider how knowledge about atoms can prove highly useful to areas entirely outside chemistry. Knowledge that electrons occupy specific energy levels in an atom might suggest a pattern useful to robust digital communication systems, whereby well-defined states beget signal integrity. Weaker bonding between atoms, which give flexibility in materials, might suggest a better approach to achieving collaboration while remaining flexible. The way outer electrons dictate atomic behavior might be the telltale signs of effective interaction protocols in highly connected systems. The arrangements seen in atomic lattices might be more broadly applicable to urban planning.

The point is, studying atoms is indeed worth it, but not to connect them causally into larger systems via design. Studying atoms is important because they showcase universal properties that nature adheres to, and analogous systems at varying scales will undoubtedly operate under similar constraints.

When it comes to the knowledge we teach future generations, we need to do away with the design narrative. The isolated pieces of knowledge that appear in textbooks are not paths to creating real world solutions, they are examples that demonstrate universally true properties; properties that many other systems will exhibit. It is knowledge of these properties paired with our natural human ability to embrace trial-and-error and think heuristically that will lead to the best solutions.

We're Supposed to be Doing Alchemy

A common criticism of today's AI research and engineering is that it looks more like alchemy than a real science. Progress in AI does not benefit much from deliberate design or reductionist thinking. It has moved forward thanks to adding more data, throwing more computing power at the problem, and mixing and matching hyperparameters in a relatively ad hoc fashion; all to the chagrin of traditional scientists and statisticians.

By now the reader should realize that such ad hoc, messy work is precisely what AI must be. AI is approaching genuine complexity, as it must to solve hard problems, and genuine complexity cannot be created through design. The fictional cause-and-effect reductionism of traditional science will not make AI better.

The success of today's AI has occurred because deep learning is based on an approach fundamentally different from traditional science, statistics and rules-based software. As with cities, electrical grids, and the market, AI does not get its most critical outputs from the deliberate designs of engineers. AI achieves its necessary internals by an external process akin to how nature creates solutions.

But as usual, the design narrative creeps its way back into the efforts of scientists and engineers. The ad-hoc nature by which today's AI engineering progresses sounds all too unsophisticated. Today's researchers want to design neural architectures and the many pieces that sit within.

But we are supposed to be doing alchemy. We are supposed to be mixing and matching things in an ad hoc fashion and waiting to see what happens. This is, in fact, far more rigorous an approach than operating under the fictions of design. Rather than pretending to have access to information it does not, the alchemical approach remains outside the systems and waits to see what happens. It lets nature converge on solutions.

Of course, alchemy never produced gold, so the analogy must stop somewhere. But the point is, stepping outside and allowing nature to converge is not unscientific; such notions are a straw man used by traditional scientists stuck in a (hopefully) dying paradigm. Part of coming full circle is embracing the same spirit that compelled our forefathers to transmute the mundane into something precious.

Redefining Rigor

It is important to be rigorous in science and engineering. Rigor is how we establish reliability and validity in what we discover and build. It ensures the human quest to make informed decisions rests on our ability to draw valid conclusions. We want to build a foundation upon which future work can be assembled. This all lends itself to the trust and credibility the public deserves, as they look to rely on the theories and inventions we produce.

But the current perception of what is considered rigorous is becoming more and more problematic. Scientists and laymen alike view harder skills as being more rigorous than something high-level and less precise. When one looks at a theory filled with mathematical equations it appears stronger than one with mere words and diagrams. Precision expressed inside formal systems makes things appear so much more concrete. But there is a cost to this precision that is conveniently ignored by our current paradigm. When we express our discoveries precisely, using mathematical symbols or causal calculations, we lose much of the context that gives things meaning.

And yet, we are causal creatures. We need to anchor what we perceive in the world onto definite things. We need to know that what we measure, observe and experience can be placed into realistic models that help us make better decisions.

I have already detailed in this book what proper rigor looks like under complexity. Is it the creation of logical arguments whose premises rest on timeless properties rather than causal reasons. But this alone does not attend to our need for causality and determinism. Yes, properties act as constraints we expect complex things to adhere to. We can use them to reason about whether we are on the right track as we build complex solutions. But they also have a kind of *connective tissue*. They are not merely distinct properties with no relation.

Let us consider a book one more time. Books have narrative structures that transition from a setup towards rising challenges, and ultimately into solutions to those challenges. As I have argued, this structure should not be used to seed or guide writing, only as after-the-fact signals that writing is going well. The different parts of the narrative structure are properties of good writing, but these properties have a meta-causal connection between them. The setup *leads into* the rising tension, which *transitions to* some climax, which eventually *flows into* some resolution.

The narrative structure of writing can be seen as an external, meta structure whose parts act as properties that are causally connected. This means that if we shift our definition of knowledge externally, away from the inner causes of things, we can salvage the kind of causality and determinism humans use to reason with.

This is a properly placed concreteness, in contrast to the misplaced concreteness that has occurred due to our reductionist scientific and engineering paradigm. When causality is used at the meta level, it becomes a formidable tool to reason about what we are building. There is structure and reason to that which exists at the meta level. This brings a much more realistic approach to being rigorous when discussing the creation of complex things.

Humanity needs to redefine rigor as that which exists externally to the systems we hope to create. This is where humans first encountered the intuitive causality and determinism our self-awareness and reason depend on. Not in the guts of deterministic systems, or the fancy symbols of our theories and explanations, but in the naturally complex world we learned to survive in. Perhaps humanity's greatest discovery will be its realization that progress, in its best form, brings us closer to where we started.

Epilogue

This book is a product of many years of building things and thinking deeply about the nature of problem solving. It is a culmination of toil and observation, long thoughtful walks and countless thought experiments. There have been many drafts I thought were *it*, only to have me iterate yet again as nature exposed unreconciled fragments or incomplete arguments. Some of the most critical insights I arrived at were felt the deepest while endeavoring to write this book.

Among my years of experience in both academia and industry I have been more frustrated than pleased with how science and engineering are conducted. I have worked and published within our reductionist paradigm, and have contributed to, and directed, large software projects for companies. The academic and design narratives were present throughout, interfering as they do.

This book represents my most important revelations regarding how nature works. Such theses are usually presented in journals, and often in mathematical form. But as the reader can guess by now, this is not the approach I deem most critical. Today's world needs legitimate commentary on science far more than it needs science itself. I hope this will not always be the case, but as we (hopefully) transition away from traditional engineering and reductionism, I see this as the greatest service one can do for science and society.

Creating is not just about bringing new things into the world. I believe the best philosophies are granted to us through the act of creation. Only by attempting to fashion things that work are we in direct communication with nature. The deepest most universal truths in life are contained in the patterns that arise when one builds things.

Philosophy and creativity should never be unbound. To divorce one from the other is to remove understanding and meaning from where truth lives. Our most important questions about existence, knowledge, values, reason and the mind live inside the constructs waiting to be made. Like Michelangelo's already-existing statue inside his untouched stone, what works in nature is already there, waiting to be discovered. If only we pick up the chisel.

This book is what remains from years of chiseling. Not just inside academic and industrial experiences, but in life itself. I have witnessed the stark contrast between creating emergently versus *by design* throughout my life. One of my favorite examples is playing piano. I do not read sheet music; I just sit down and play. I look at the keys and create music in the moment. I do not see this as anything special, but many others do, including those trained as pianists. The trained pianist knows the specifics, the details, the best practices. But they almost never compose their own music, and many stop playing later in life. When I see the lessoned player perform, I see rigid movement and forced inflexibility. The pianist appears artificially occupied, looking back and forth between sheet music and keys, as though they're doing everything to stop the piano from falling apart. It does not look enjoyable, and I am willing to bet that for many, it is not.

The same can be said for mathematics. The awkward and rigid movements seen in piano lessons parallels the lifeless symbol manipulation forced upon students. The boredom and difficulty found in so many of today's endeavors are a direct result of the academic and design narratives. Fundamentals are the last thing you should learn. Humans are meant to experience the emergence of structure and behavior through naive trial-and-error, not isolated concepts devoid of context. Our work is meant to be enjoyable, for joy signals that the deep complexities of our natural abilities are being used.

There is no great mystery to being creative or showcasing skill. Composing music on the spot, building a software prototype in one sitting, inventing a new theory; these are not end results of serious training or instruction, these come from placing oneself into the mess of life, and allowing nature to *reveal* what works. We should all be moving our fingers haphazardly across the keys of life, to discover nature's statue inside.

I will end by reflecting on the content of this book, to summarize its key points and themes. I began by stating that society requires a fundamental change in mindset. That we must realize, and accept, that the approach used to build things in today's economy is coming to an end. Today's challenges cannot be solved using simple systems. As we continue to add more pieces to what we build we run into harder problems, and eventually the need for complex solutions.

The designs of yesterday were based on rules. Our forefathers created deterministic connections between their current state and the next level of physical abstraction. This has moved humanity forward technologically, but it also brought us up against categorically different problems; naturally hard problems. These cannot be resolved by inner reasoning and determinism, for those are the stuff of design. Design, as I have argued, cannot work to resolve our biggest challenges.

But progress by abstraction is absolute. Abstraction is how nature finds answers inside astronomically large possibility spaces. A more difficult problem cannot be solved by merely connecting more pieces together into a different object. Pieces must be bundled into higher-level constructs for the next generation to use. For humans to continue making progress we must learn to raise the level of abstraction as nature does.

This means learning to build genuinely complex solutions, and engineering the emergent properties that compute answers to hard problems. We know such things are possible. Our cities, financial systems, electrical grids, the internet and artificial intelligence systems all produce their most critical outputs through emergent behavior, not design.

But our current paradigm does not accept the building of complex things. Today's science and engineering sees emergence as an exception to an otherwise orderly and reductionist world. We still operate under the faulty assumption that there are causal paths to what we see; paths we can engineer ourselves into new solutions.

Nature's true sophistication shows us this is not the case. Human invention pales in comparison to nature's solutions. Human innovation is more a story of forcing the natural world to adhere to the low dimensionality of our creations than to some astounding level of human achievement.

The real achievement is the high-level process of invention itself. While our creations to date have been mostly simple and deterministic, the human capacity to envision possibilities and find ways to survive is timeless. The credit goes to nature. We evolved to maneuver through highly complex environments and think heuristically. The age of complexity brings us full circle, as we learn to embrace our most natural skills to operate in our modern economy.

The biggest shift science and engineering needs to embrace is a move from internal to external processes. The inner causal reasoning that makes design possible must now be replaced by external meta knowledge. Only external processes that fully admit epistemic barriers and indecipherability can create solutions that work under complexity. The flexible determinism needed to compute answers to hard problems only materializes when we step outside the systems we hope to create.

Complexity, with its emergent structures and behaviors, is not some niche area of nature, or just one of many disciplines worth studying. Emergence *is* nature. From the atom to the ant colony, nature manifests configurations of matter that compute answers to hard problems. This is why the rifle is simpler than the helium atom. Whereas the rifle produces its outputs using simple cause-and-effect actions, helium is a different entity than anything a sum of neutrons, protons and electrons can define.

When viewed through the lens of information, computing and evolution we can see that nature's patterns are the reflections of problem structure. Nature poses problems through environmental stressors, and those problems have nested definitions that must be resolved by levels of emergence. These levels reside within nature's solutions, which we perceive as hierarchical nested structures. Such structures are nature's version of physical abstraction, created the only way abstractions can be; by a self-referencing meta process that produces invariance.

Nature achieves far higher levels of meta than we do with our inventions, because her targets are *on the surface*. Nature never reaches into the guts of systems and designs her internals. We must learn to keep our problem statements general and our pieces flexible. Only then will our trial-and-error efforts remain tractable.

Nature is not a game, yet the overwhelming amount of science and engineering at work today operates as though it is. Our techniques use the supposed rigor of mathematics and causal theories to attach to things unreal. We do not need fancy mathematics or causal explanations to know nature, we need high-level rational arguments based on known properties of complexity.

Our world currently runs on design. We celebrate the detail-oriented, while denigrating softer skills. This leads to cherry picking over group selection, straw man arguments that unscientifically chalk complexity up to magic, an irrational belief in genius, and a backwards education system that does anything but prepare students for tomorrow.

The reality is tomorrow's world will not see fundamentals precede application. The direction of complexity holds under all natural environments. Despite the human need for causal explanations, the patterns we observe in nature are not the paths to get there.

Science and engineering need to become a single discipline because building things is the best way to discover new truths. Further, the discoveries of science are best used as meta knowledge that helps us validate, after-the-fact, that we are building the right things. The isolation and extraction of today's research experiments cannot map to a realistic picture of nature. But the act of building things contains all the information we could hope to glean.

Humans already have all the skills they need to build in the age of complexity. We evolved to solve hard problems, not simplistic ones. What has allowed us to survive is what will enable us to build genuine complexity and engineer emergence.

Design, as a concept, need not be tossed out. Humans can make decisions about how to set up projects and validate work, as long as we *shift up*, and design externally. Only meta-design is valid in the age of complexity.

We need a new education system. One that rewards group activity over "smart" students. One that does not run under the premise of design, but instead sees isolated textbook knowledge as examples of universally true properties, rather than ways to produce things that work. One that engenders rational argument and critical thinking, without the hidden and false premise that small things lead directly to big things. One that teaches the meta structures found in nature's solutions, and how to validate work in the same direction complexity runs.

Human bias, high-level thinking and soft skills are what work under complexity. They exist in us because they are what led to survival. Tomorrow's challenges will have more in common with running into bears and scraping our way through forests than piecing together office buildings, bridges, internal combustion engines and rockets. These things will still be built, but if all goes well, they will be built differently.

We must not look upon details as though they are a more rigorous account of what is. For true rigor rests on things undeniable, and there is nothing more undeniable than the invariant truths that have stood the test of time.

To build is to reign-in the mess of nature and refashion something that works for our survival. It is our most human attribute. Perhaps only now are we on the precipice of embracing humanity's true potential.

Index

A

academics, 251

adaptive, 2, 55, 113, 260

after-the-fact, 170, 172, 227, 273, 279, 283, 285, 293, 301

age of complexity, 4, 5, 29, 48, 82, 91, 92, 110, 140, 142, 169, 182, 187, 192, 209, 214, 215, 216, 218, 227, 228, 257, 258, 274, 279, 299, 301, 302

aggregation, 31, 36, 37, 136

AI, xiii, xiv, 16, 26, 37, 38, 41, 42, 45, 46, 47, 54, 55, 78, 113, 124, 125, 126, 129, 133, 134, 135, 136, 138, 143, 184, 187, 188, 189, 196, 202, 205, 206, 245, 246, 247, 248, 249, 250, 253, 259, 261, 262, 263, 269, 274, 279, 291

alchemy, 46, 189, 291, 292

algorithms, 43, 61, 62, 69, 73, 81, 112, 135, 139, 184, 254, 255

analogy, 19, 27, 38, 61, 118, 119, 292

analysis, 75, 76, 77, 81, 87, 121, 126, 226, 246

analytical, 60, 76, 123, 137, 257

ancestors, 18, 47, 73, 219

approximation, 26, 27, 83, 104, 109, 181, 195, 265

architectures, 44, 125, 135, 139, 291

argument, 49, 163, 164, 165, 176, 186, 223, 225, 240, 241, 246, 264, 278, 302

attachability, 181

attributes, 69, 107, 118, 149, 198

autocomplete, 270

automatic, 13, 20, 21, 31, 57, 120, 134, 142, 149, 172, 177, 237

automatically, 57, 59, 60, 64, 65, 120, 125, 132, 148, 163, 273

automobile, 19, 52, 53, 113, 122, 213

B

bad science, 166

behaviors, 24, 35, 36, 37, 86, 93, 101, 103, 104, 110, 114, 119, 120, 127, 134, 154, 156, 169, 191, 194, 197, 205, 221, 227, 233, 242, 255, 261, 274, 279, 287, 299

bias, 5, 83, 186, 190, 201, 280, 281, 302

biological, 42, 60, 63, 99, 132, 133, 136, 160, 162, 167, 272, 288

bodybuilders, 219, 220

F

factors, 11, 25, 26, 30, 32, 56, 68, 86, 88, 113, 159, 239, 246

feature space, 69, 70, 71, 72, 73

features, 60, 62, 69, 70, 71, 72, 74, 118, 124, 133, 178, 256

flexible, 59, 85, 86, 88, 90, 111, 113, 138, 139, 140, 168, 178, 196, 200, 203, 260, 290, 299, 300

flexible determinism, 86, 90, 111

fragile, 154, 216, 219, 272

framework, 23, 24, 99, 124, 164, 169, 182, 183, 184, 190, 194

functionalities, 22, 108

functions, 14, 39, 52, 60, 64, 91, 132, 135, 138, 139, 158, 161, 193, 200, 207, 229, 236, 242, 256, 260, 262, 272

fundamental, 1, 28, 44, 48, 82, 131, 185, 186, 225, 254, 263, 276, 286, 297

G

gamifying, 203, 234

generation, 12, 14, 15, 17, 18, 19, 20, 21, 29, 32, 57, 119, 227, 271, 272, 285, 298

generations, 12, 16, 56, 57, 196, 228, 290

genius, 234, 301

genuine complexity, 33, 136, 259, 272, 279, 291, 301

Gödel's incompleteness, 207

going meta, 121, 123, 126, 130, 131

group, 22, 56, 106, 116, 121, 123, 130, 132, 139, 143, 144, 145, 146, 147, 148, 150, 168, 170, 218, 219, 229, 235, 237, 244, 280, 281, 301, 302

H

heuristics, 5, 25, 75, 76, 77, 79, 81, 83, 87, 109, 137, 173, 174, 186, 187, 188, 234, 249, 263, 270, 272, 285

hierarchies, 56

high-dimensional, 41, 70, 71, 200, 256, 257

higher-level, 15, 17, 19, 22, 23, 29, 30, 31, 44, 62, 89, 99, 105, 127, 130, 153, 207, 227, 235, 244, 298

high-level, 18, 39, 42, 49, 59, 79, 84, 87, 97, 123, 128, 139, 154, 161, 174, 187, 188, 189, 214, 216, 234, 243, 272, 293, 299, 301, 302

human history, 1, 4, 64, 111, 117, 278

humanity, 6, 7, 13, 21, 32, 270, 285, 294, 298, 302

I

implementing, 18, 39, 88

indecipherable, 80, 84

individuals, 16, 47, 56, 83, 144, 146, 153, 166, 198, 216, 217, 218, 235, 236, 280, 281

Industrial Revolution, 5, 185, 285

inevitable, 13, 17, 21, 49, 120, 127, 129, 149, 156, 176, 177, 178, 237, 259, 261

information, 13, 19, 30, 36, 38, 41, 42, 44, 45, 48, 58, 61, 63,

K

N

O

T

About the Author

Sean McClure is an independent scholar and entrepreneur at the intersection of science, complexity, and philosophy. His blend of academic and industry experience stimulated his current commentary on the intellectual climate of our times. Sean holds a Ph.D. in Computational Chemistry, composes piano music in his spare time, and enjoys long walks.

www.ingramcontent.com/pod-product-compliance
Lightning Source LLC
Chambersburg PA
CBHW031431060726
47600CB00002B/10